Teacher's ELL Handbook
Strategies for English Language Learners

Needham, Massachusetts
Upper Saddle River, New Jersey
Glenview, Illinois

Nancy Vincent Montgomery, Ed. D., has worked with English Language Learners for 30 years, beginning upon her graduation from Southern Illinois University in Carbondale, Illinois, with a Bachelor of Science degree in education. While teaching she was awarded two education grants to implement literacy projects with English Language Learners and was honored with a Teacher of the Year award. Her pursuit of two Master's degrees and a doctorate in education allowed her to continue her research in second language writing, literacy, and assessment. In addition, her many opportunities to visit other countries and study their cultures helped her to gain a true understanding of the complexities of learning a new language and a new culture. She has taught at an international school in Asia, and has completed field research in schools in Africa, Asia, Europe, and Latin America. She is currently a senior consultant for a Language and Literacy Cooperative in Dallas, Texas, where she resides.

ISBN 0-13-058536-X

1 2 3 4 5 6 7 8 9 10 05 04 03 02 01

Contents

To the Teacher

In the past decade there have been an increasing number of students entering U.S. public schools from multiple linguistic and cultural backgrounds. The number of Americans identifying themselves as Hispanic, for example, grew by nearly 60 percent since the 1990 census, roughly three million people more than predicted by the Census Bureau. The unexpected increase in the population of people from non-English-speaking cultures presents a major challenge for our schools: to create an optimal learning environment that will ensure comprehension for every student in all content areas of the curriculum.

This Handbook and Prentice Hall's *Science Explorer* program can help you meet this challenge. As you know, English Language Learners face a number of language-related obstacles to learning that are compounded by the specialized nature of content area subjects. For example, English Language Learners with little or no experience using English text will find it difficult to move from narrative to expository text and to develop hypotheses and make inferences from a textbook. The more sophisticated sentence structure of middle school materials and the need for more advanced study skills at this level contribute to the difficulty of understanding content material. Science, in particular, can prove difficult for the English Language Learner due to its technical vocabulary and the student's limited prior knowledge.

Teachers of ELL students face their own challenges. For instance, the language skills of ELL students can vary widely. Students who have been in our schools three years or less may still be acquiring Basic Interpersonal Communication Skills (BICS). Other students who have been in our schools five years or longer may have developed BICS but are still acquiring Cognitive Academic Language Proficiency Skills (CALPS). Even those students who have attained a high level of CALPS may need additional language support through second-language strategies.

Understanding the part that BICS and CALPS play in the comprehension of concepts will help the content-area teacher when teaching students with varying English language skills. The four language skills—reading, writing, speaking, and listening—need to be developed along with the specialized content area material for ELL students to completely comprehend a subject. These students also need sheltered instruction to be successful, because they often have limited schooling experience and background knowledge of the content area, and lack technical and specialized vocabulary.

Using This Handbook

Since the key to teaching ELL students is in presenting comprehensible material, awareness of the oral language proficiency level of your students and the strategies that will effectively meet their needs is most important. The Oral Language Proficiency Chart (on page 9) summarizes the characteristics of each level of language, instructional ideas for teachers, and performance indicators for students. The chart is followed by detailed explanations of each level of language. General strategies for the teacher and student, graphic organizers that are appropriate for English Language Learners, and vocabulary and comprehension strategies are also included in this handbook. Transparencies of the graphic organizers are included for use as starting points. Also, alternative methods of assessment for ELL students at all levels of language proficiency are suggested.

The later pages of the Handbook show how the pedagogy and features of *Science Explorer* aid the success of the English Language Learner. These pages also contain sample lessons from *Science Explorer* books on life, earth, and physical science that show how to apply the strategies in this Handbook to the content of all lessons.

Language Proficiency Levels

Like all content areas, science can prove difficult for English Language Learners. The specialized vocabulary and complexity of the subject matter, coupled with students' typically scant prior knowledge of science and limited English proficiency, can cause frustration for ELL students and for teachers who need to reach all students. Science teachers, therefore, need to be familiar with the levels of oral language proficiency and with some instructional tools that will make scientific material comprehensible for the English Language Learner. This information is outlined in the chart on page 9 and explained in more detail below.

There are five levels of oral language proficiency. Levels I and II are considered beginning levels. Levels III and IV are intermediate levels, and Level V is the advanced, or transitional, level. Each level has distinct characteristics that have implications for instruction.

Characteristics of the English Language Learner: Beginning Level

- The beginning-level student has minimal to very limited comprehension of the English language. It is important to realize that this student is acquiring Basic Interpersonal Communication Skills (BICS), which can take up to three years.

- Student's speech will range from nothing to one or two individual words to phrases of two or three words.

- Many students at this level go through a silent period, in which they do not speak or even attempt to speak. This stage is common and can last from just a few hours to three months or perhaps longer. Keep in mind that these students are listening, observing, and learning language, even though it may appear that they are not. In fact, they may know some English but be too shy to speak. Verbalization depends on the individual student and his or her prior experiences with school. Do not force students to speak during this time. Allow them to speak their native language with one another or with you, if possible, for clarification of information.

What Beginning-Level Students Can Do: Performance Indicators

- Students can point to responses.

- They can label diagrams, illustrations, and maps. Many students who can neither speak nor comprehend English can illustrate a concept and label a map or diagram if they are given a sample. This activity gives students practice writing in English and helps them connect English words to a visual.

- They can use "yes" and "no" cards, gestures, manipulatives, or lab equipment to show understanding.

Instructional Ideas for Teachers of Beginning-Level Students

- Focus on vocabulary building through the use of visuals and concrete objects.

- Develop concepts through the use of graphic organizers, but keep them simple; beginning-level students can easily become confused and frustrated with graphic organizers that have many lines or circles.

- Play games that require nonverbal responses; for example, games in which students match words to pictures or diagrams. Students can also use "yes" and "no" cards to indicate understanding. Any activities that require nonverbal responses are called Total Physical Response activities.

- Give students an opportunity to build comprehension by developing open-ended sentences using words the students already know, words from a word bank, and words posted in the classroom.

Characteristics of the English Language Learner: Intermediate Level

- There is a noticeable increase in the student's comprehension.
- The student's sentence structure varies from simple to complex.
- The student is able to engage in conversation at a deeper level.
- The student's errors in speech vary from simple to complex. The student moves beyond the present tense and uses plurals with ease.
- Students at this level are attaining or have attained Cognitive Academic Language Proficiency Skills (CALPS).

What Intermediate-Level Students Can Do: Performance Indicators

- Students can use complete sentences ranging in structure from simple to complex.
- They participate in class discussions more easily and at a deeper level.
- They integrate higher-order thinking skills, such as debating, evaluating, and analyzing, into group discussions.

Instructional Ideas for Teachers of Intermediate-Level Students

- Use higher-level graphic organizers and visuals.
- Structure group discussions to encourage students to speak.
- Use Cloze activities (discussed on page 18) for vocabulary and concept building.
- Structure questions that require complete answers to encourage higher-order thinking skills.

Characteristics of the English Language Learner: Advanced Level

- The student is nearly proficient in English speech.
- The student has a higher level of comprehension.
- The student may lack writing experience in his or her native language as well as in English.
- The student's vocabulary may be near the level of a native speaker.
- Students at this level have attained a high level of Cognitive Academic Language Proficiency Skills (CALPS).

What Advanced-Level Students Can Do: Performance Indicators

- Students incorporate higher-order thinking skills in writing and speaking.
- Their participation in problem solving is near the level of participation of native speakers.
- They use more advanced vocabulary in debates, discussions, or other situations involving intensive communications.
- They show little hesitancy to speak.
- They do not require as many instructional modifications.
- They can complete all performance indicators listed on the Oral Language Proficiency Chart.

Instructional Ideas for Teachers of Advanced-Level Students

- Continue vocabulary building throughout lessons.
- Continue providing opportunities for students to use higher-order thinking skills.
- Integrate writing as well as reading into lessons, as many transitional students will be weak in writing skills.

Oral Language Proficiency Chart

Levels of Proficiency	Level I	Level II	Level III	Level IV	Level V (Transitional)
	Pre-Production Stage	Early Production Stage	Speech Emergence	Intermediate Fluency Stage	Near Proficient
ELL CATEGORIES	Beginning		Intermediate		Advanced
Characteristics of the English Language Learner	• Minimal comprehension • May be very shy • No verbal production • Non-English speaker • Silent period (10 hours to 3 months) • Uses gestures and actions to communicate	• Limited comprehension • Gives one- or two-word responses • May use two- or three-word phrases • Stage may last 6 months to 2 years	• Comprehension increases • Errors still occur in speech • Simple sentences • Stage may last 2 to 4 years	• Good comprehension • Sentences become more complex • Engages in conversation • Errors in speech are more complex	• Few errors in speech • Orally proficient • Near-native vocabulary • Lacks writing skill • Uses complex sentences
What They Can Do: Performance Indicators	• Listen • Point • Illustrate • Match • Choose	• Name • List and group • Categorize • Label • Demonstrate	• Compare and contrast • Recall and retell • Summarize • Explain	• Higher-order thinking skills • Analyze, debate, justify	• All performance indicators
Instructional Ideas for Teachers	• Visual cues • Tape passages • Pair students • Total Physical Response activities • Concrete objects • Graphic organizers	• Short homework assignments • Short-answer quizzes • Open-ended sentences	• Graphs • Tables • Group discussions • Student-created books • Cloze activities	• Group panels • Paraphrasing • Defending and debating	• Lessons on writing mechanics • Free reading of appropriate books • Cooperative learning groups

Strategies for Relating to English Language Learners

There are a number of basic strategies teachers can implement to meet the needs of their English Language Learners. In fact, these are common-sense, everyday strategies that teachers in all content areas already know and use. These strategies lay the foundation for a positive learning relationship between the student and the teacher.

Simplify Your Teacher Talk

One of the most important strategies is modifying and simplifying your "teacher talk," or the way you speak to your students during instruction. Often the vocabulary and sentence structure that teachers use are beyond the comprehension of their students. To avoid this problem, speak directly and succinctly, using simple words and sentences with students who are at a beginning-language level. Since ELL students are learning a new language as well as new academic concepts, avoid using slang or idiomatic expressions, which can add to their confusion. Using body language to emphasize important words or rephrasing a sentence or definition will also aid the English Language Learner in understanding new information.

Learn About Your Students' Heritage

You do not need to be able to speak a second language in order to make your ELL students feel you are interested in them. Learn as much as you can about the cultures and languages represented by the students in your classroom. Not only will you increase your own knowledge, but you will enhance the self-esteem of your students as they become aware of your interest in their heritage. You can also use your knowledge to broaden the horizons of the English-speaking students in your class.

Limited English Proficiency Does Not Mean Limited Thinking Skills

English Language Learners possess higher-order thinking skills, but many times it is believed that because the students are not proficient in English, they do not have those skills. Encourage hypothesizing, analyzing, inferring, justifying, and making predictions, as well as other thinking skills. Students need opportunities to observe and use these skills in the classroom, as explained in the various strategy sections of this handbook.

Give ELL Students Time to Respond

Increase response "wait time" for English Language Learners. These students must process information in two languages and will respond more quickly in a relaxed, risk-free environment. Then repeat the student's response in a natural manner in standard English. Repeating the response correctly will validate the student's response.

Give ELL Students a Sneak Preview

Provide an outline or list of instructions and review these with your ELL students. Give them an opportunity to look ahead in the text or view a model of the assignment. By doing so, you also inform students of your expectations.

Watch for Nonverbal Signals

English Language Learners use a number of nonverbal signals to show lack of understanding. These may include lowering the head, avoiding eye contact, covering the assignment paper, or simply a general look of confusion. Watch for these signs and be prepared to provide individual attention or assign the student to a partner in the classroom for help.

Provide a Risk-Free Learning Environment

Many English Language Learners come from cultures in which they were taught not to question the teacher, critique the information presented, or in general request clarification, simplification, or repetition. Some ELL students do not ask for help because their lack of English language proficiency makes them feel uncomfortable. Often these students will nod their head in agreement, smile, and appear to understand exactly what you are saying—until their test results prove otherwise.

Be prepared to teach students that it is acceptable to ask questions and critique information presented. At the same time try to provide a risk-free environment that will foster student questioning, no matter what their level of language proficiency. Help your students view you as being sensitive to their needs and as someone who will provide guidance in understanding content material.

Allow Students to Use Their Native Language

Let students know that it is acceptable to use their native language in the classroom. One way is to allow students to use their native language during student-to-student collaboration. Because many ELL students feel that their native language is not valued, you may want to use your knowledge of the students' language in instruction. This not only helps those students with very limited English proficiency, but also shows acceptance and appreciation of the students' native language.

Vocabulary Instruction for English Language Learners

Vocabulary can be particularly difficult for the English Language Learner, especially in science, because science vocabulary is usually technical and specialized. ELL students come from a variety of schooling backgrounds and may have limited experience with science. To complicate matters, many English words have more than one meaning, depending on the context in which they are used.

Take the word *table*, for example. In common English usage, the word *table* refers to a piece of furniture with legs and a flat horizontal surface. But in science, a table is a display of data in columns and rows. Often ELL students will translate an English word into their native language based on the most common usage of the word. For example, Spanish-speaking students may translate *table* as *mesa*, the piece of furniture. Or they may expect the English word to be similar to the word in their native language, in which case they may translate *table* as *tabla*, and then proceed to interpret it as *board* instead of *chart*. Because of these factors, teachers should use instructional strategies such as the ones below when introducing ELL students to new vocabulary.

Instructional Strategies

Relate New Words to Past and Present Experiences

Vocabulary instruction is most effective when it links new vocabulary to the background knowledge and experiences of the students as well as to words and concepts students are studying at the time. Associating new words with past and present learning experiences and showing the connection between the words and real life will improve students' comprehension. You can use direct questioning techniques to find out which words the students have already learned and how they learned them. If students lack background knowledge in a specific area, then you should build background before presenting content material.

Teaching a word out of context (that is, in isolation) can be effective, however, if the instruction involves motivating the student's interest in the word through visuals, demonstrating the use of the word, and showing a connection between the student and the word.

Make a Science Glossary

Allow students to make their own science glossaries as new words are introduced. This will give them practice reading and writing the word and will provide them with a reference. Briefly define each word. Invite students to draw a picture of the word, to include examples of synonyms, and to write the word in their native language if needed.

Provide Conversational Opportunities

Provide your English Language Learners with meaningful conversational opportunities in a risk-free environment. One strategy is to place students in cooperative groups, which gives them an opportunity to interact verbally with other students and to practice English sounds.

When designing cooperative grouping for the science classroom, do not place all English Language Learners in the same group. Their vocabulary skills will improve faster if they are integrated throughout the class with native English speakers. It is best, however, not to place beginning-level ELL students with the most advanced English speakers. Instead, place beginning ELL students with average achievers and intermediate or advanced ELL students with high achievers.

Use New Vocabulary in Writing and Homework Assignments

Design writing assignments so that students practice using the new words. Students need to develop a feel for how the vocabulary looks in writing, as well as how it sounds when spoken. Seeing the vocabulary written down helps students understand the structure and patterns of the English language. These assignments will help students develop good writing skills as well as foster vocabulary growth. For many English Language Learners, English may be their second spoken language, but their first written language.

Include the new vocabulary in take-home class assignments as well, so that vocabulary will be used outside of class. This reinforces the use of the new words and shows the relevance of the words to daily life. In addition, give students permission to incorporate illustrations of vocabulary words in writing assignments, class work, and homework. This is especially important for the beginning-level student.

Teach Independent Word-Analysis Strategies

Teach students word-analysis strategies so that new words can be attacked independently. For example, teach the prefix and/or suffix and the root of the designated vocabulary word. Write the meaning of the prefix and/or suffix and the root word on the board and have students do the same in their science glossaries. By providing this information whenever a new word is presented, students learn how to decode unfamiliar words and at the same time add new information to their glossaries for future reference. Teaching word-analysis skills also helps students understand how language works—knowledge that cannot be assumed, since English Language Learners come from all levels of schooling and background experiences.

Provide Independent Reading Opportunities

Have available in the classroom independent reading materials that relate to the content being studied and that use the new vocabulary words. These materials give students the opportunity to see the words used in context but in a leisure reading or research setting. Independent reading material might include trade and reference books as well as picture books that are interesting and age appropriate.

Increase Students' Exposure to New Words

Give students as much exposure as possible to new vocabulary words. The following paragraphs describe how.

- Post the words on a Word Wall in patterns that are easy for students to recognize. For example, words can be arranged in alphabetical order, in word families (such as by prefix or suffix), or organized by topic or concept. English Language Learners should understand how the words were chosen and how they relate to the content being studied. The Word Wall must also be an interactive instructional tool. Refer to the words often, use them in instruction, and assign them in homework to validate their study.

- Use the words in a graphic organizer. Many types of graphic organizers are appropriate for vocabulary study. The most important consideration is that the graphic organizer reflect the language level of the learner. A graphic organizer that is too complex will easily confuse the beginning-level English Language Learner. Likewise, a very simple graphic organizer will not be effective for ELL students who are at the advanced level.

- Incorporate new vocabulary words into daily instruction. Modeling the use of new words allows students to hear those words pronounced correctly and in the proper context. It teaches students how to determine meanings based on semantic and syntactic clues. It also validates the study of the words. If these words are used throughout the instruction, students realize they must be important.

- Display photographs, illustrations, or physical examples of the words being taught. English Language Learners can more accurately internalize the meaning of a word if they are able to see a visual representation of it. Allow students to draw their own pictures of what words mean. From their drawings you should be able to infer how much prior knowledge they have and how much background information must be presented before moving on to new material.

- Students must see the assigned words in the text they are using in the classroom. Go through the text and point out the vocabulary words being studied so that students are aware that the new words appear in the assigned texts.

In summary, vocabulary acquisition by English Language Learners is best accomplished when the students are given opportunities to see, hear, and illustrate the words, to categorize them, to connect them to what is being studied, and to connect them to real life.

Choosing the Words You Teach

You will need to provide English Language Learners with explicit prior instruction on a limited number of technical vocabulary words related to the topic they are going to study. The number of words you preteach depends on the language levels represented in the classroom. But how do you decide which words are most important for students to know? Use the following steps to help you choose.

1. First, assess students' prior knowledge of the topic using a graphic organizer or by direct questioning. Find out how much students already know about the topic before addressing specific vocabulary words.

2. Decide which vocabulary words are important for understanding the topic. Choose vocabulary words that can be represented visually, especially for the beginning- and intermediate-level students. The words should be crucial to understanding the text and are especially good choices if the words illustrate a common point such as the use of a prefix, suffix, or root word.

3. Check to see which words students will encounter again and again in the science text. These words should be taught first. Make sure that key vocabulary is aligned with the expected learner outcomes.

4. Assess students' prior knowledge of the chosen vocabulary. Brainstorm by putting students into groups and listing the words they already know about the topic to be taught. This should give you some indication of the level of knowledge the students already have of the new vocabulary. (Remember to integrate beginning-level ELL students with native English speakers. Little brainstorming in English will take place in a group of all non-native speakers.)

5. Finally, ask yourself, What must I do as a teacher to make this vocabulary comprehensible to all of my students?

Sample Vocabulary Strategies

The following are several basic vocabulary strategies that can be used with both ELL students and English speakers.

List-Group-Label

List-Group-Label is a good vocabulary brainstorming activity for the English Language Learner. Students work in groups to list, group, and label words related to the topic being taught using the criteria in the box on the following page. Students will be more productive if they are grouped heterogeneously rather than by language levels. When students are grouped heterogeneously, they hear English spoken at different levels of proficiency, and they are more apt to participate than when they are grouped with students of the same language level.

When the groups have completed their lists, a student from each group reads the list and explains to the rest of the class why the words were grouped and labeled as they were. For a variation of this strategy, begin by providing students with one list of words and have students label and group them.

Criteria for List-Group-Label

List: Think of any word or words that remind you of the topic.

Group: Review the list of words and then group them in some way. Each group must contain at least three words, and words may appear in more than one group.

Label: Think of a title that indicates the shared relationship between the words.

Building a Science Glossary

Building a science glossary helps English Language Learners see how language works. This strategy is designed for students to work independently, but pair grouping is beneficial for students who are non-English speakers.

Choose the words for this strategy, and have visuals available for each word. Model how to divide each word into parts (prefix, root word, suffix), determine the meaning of the word, pronounce the word with and without the prefix or suffix, then use the word in a sentence. Post a list of common prefixes and suffixes in the room. This will enable your students to determine meanings on their own during independent work. The students can then add the words to their science glossary, placing the words in alphabetical order as they are added.

The English Language Learners will come to regard their glossaries as more important than the classroom dictionary because the glossaries provide not only a pronunciation and definition, but a picture of what the word means as well. The glossary also reinforces the use of the English alphabet, which is important, as not all ELL students have a solid basis in the English alphabet.

How Do I Analyze a Word?

The following strategy gives students practice comparing and contrasting vocabulary words used in the text. Students list items that are similar to and different from the vocabulary word, and then tell in which way the item is similar to or different from the given word. Since these lists will often need research, this strategy gives students practice using reference materials. Model this strategy and then give groups or pairs the opportunity to complete it independently.

Word Analysis Chart

Word(s): seismic waves

Define or rename: (text definition or teacher-led definition)

Compare

sound vibrations – pressure
   waves of air
ripples on a pond – outward
   in all directions

Contrast

ocean wave – moves up
   and down, never side to
   side or outward from a
   center

What does it look like? (student illustration)

What Do I Know About the Word?

Place students into heterogeneous language-level groups of two or three at the most. Have each group draw a T-chart on a sheet of paper. (A T-chart consists of a horizontal line across the top of the page and a vertical line down the middle.) Have students label the left column "What I Know" and the right column "What I Have Learned."

Give students a word that they are going to study in the assigned selection. Have students list what they already know about the word in the left column. After studying the selection, have students revisit the chart and add what they have learned about the word to the right column. When they have finished, discuss with students what they have learned about the selected word. From the charts and the discussion, you should get a good idea of how well students understand the vocabulary word.

Topic: Earthquakes

What I Know	What I Have Learned
Earth moves	Fractured rocks
Destroy a house	Energy carried by seismic waves
Injure or kill people	Triggered by rocks under stress

Comprehension Strategies for English Language Learners

The goal of every teacher is to make the material he or she is teaching comprehensible for all students. Teachers of English Language Learners can accomplish this goal by eliminating linguistic features of the text that will impede students' comprehension. In some cases, this means clarifying the text by adding language or rewriting sentences using simpler vocabulary. In other cases, it means supplementing the text with visual and audio aids while teaching ELL students specific reading strategies to improve comprehension. In all cases, adapting and modifying the text is key to developing students' oral and written comprehension skills. Following are some general guidelines for making the text more accessible for ELL students.

General Guidelines

1. Review the text and choose the important passages for your students to read.

   - Keep the length of the passages short—one to three paragraphs that emphasize the main points of the selection.

   - Use the Language Proficiency Chart on page 9 to help you decide how much the students can comprehend at their language level.

2. Have visual support available. Visuals give context to the selection, aid in comprehension of the text, and remind the readers of what they have read.

3. Quickly locate and analyze words that will be difficult for your students. Preteach this vocabulary so the students will have fewer obstacles as they read the text.

4. During discussions, occasionally substitute simpler vocabulary for content-based vocabulary. For example, use *windpipe* and *trachea* interchangeably for the benefit of the ELL students.

5. Whatever visuals, modification techniques, and oral instruction you use should relate to the material in the text.

Specific Comprehension Strategies

The following are some specific strategies you can use to improve the reading comprehension of your ELL students.

Cloze Strategy

The Cloze strategy can be used for pre- and post-assessments as well as During Reading comprehension checks. This exercise will help you determine not only the extent of your students' vocabulary but how well they comprehend what they read. Below are some guidelines that can be used to develop a Cloze for the English Language Learner.

1. Choose a passage for your students to read that is at the appropriate language level.

2. Leave the first and last sentences intact, but delete important words from the sentences in between. The first and last sentences are left because they are usually introductory and concluding sentences, and they help the students determine out the meaning of the missing words.

3. The difficulty of the deleted words must correspond to the language levels of the students in the classroom. Have students read or review the passage and use one of the following methods to replace the words that have been deleted:

   - Write in words from a teacher-provided word bank
   - Draw pictures that represent the deleted words
   - Choose from two words in parentheses; the correct answer could range from obvious (for the beginning ELL student) to subtle (for the advanced student)

Cloze Strategy Models

These models are appropriate for beginning- to intermediate-level English Language Learners. The vocabulary used is taken directly from the paragraph in the book, so the student is not expected to call up vocabulary that is not yet acquired.

Model I

Fill in the blanks with word-bank words.

Feathers

The rule is this: If it has feathers, it's a bird. _*Feathers*_ probably evolved from reptiles' scales. Both feathers and _*scales*_ are made of the same tough material as your fingernails. _*Birds*_ have several types of feathers. If you've ever picked up a _*feather*_ from the ground, chances are good that it was a contour feather. A contour feather is one of the large feathers that give shape to a bird's body.

Word Bank: feathers reptiles scales birds feather

Model II

Fill in the blanks with one of the words in parentheses.

Types of Rock

Some kinds of rock weather more rapidly than others. The minerals that make up the _____rock_____ (rock, water) determine how fast it _____weathers_____ (dissolves, weathers). Rock made of _____minerals_____ (water, minerals) that dissolve easily in water weathers faster. Some _____rocks_____ (rocks, trees) weather easily because they are permeable. _____Permeable_____ (Weathering, Permeable) means that a material is full of tiny, connected air spaces that allow water to seep through it. Permeable rock weathers chemically at a fast rate.

QAR (Question-Answer Relationship) Strategy

In this strategy, English Language Learners learn about four types of questions, ranging from literal to analytical, and how to respond to each type. The strategy and vocabulary a student uses to answer a question will allow the teacher to determine the student's level of comprehension. The strategies are described below.

In the Book If the answer to the question can be found in the text, the student will use one of two In the Book strategies to formulate the answer.

1. **Right There:** The words used to formulate the question are taken directly from the text, so that the answer is "right there."

In the Book: Right There Model

Sample Text
Oxygen and nitrogen together make up 99 percent of dry air. Carbon dioxide and argon make up most of the other 1 percent. The **remaining gases are called trace gases** because only small amounts of them are present.

Question: Why are the **remaining gases in dry air called trace gases**?

Answer Strategy: **In the Book: Right There**

Because the question was formed by restating a sentence from the

---

text, students can find the answer to the question "right there," in the text. This is an example of a literal question and answer. This type of question would be appropriate for those students who are at the beginning or near intermediate level of English proficiency.

2. **Think and Search:** The answer can be found in the text, but it is spread over several sentences or paragraphs. The students must "think" about what the question is asking, then "search" the text for the answer.

In the Book: Think and Search Model

> **Sample Text**
> Oxygen and nitrogen together make up 99 percent of dry air. Carbon dioxide and argon make up most of the other 1 percent. The remaining gases are called trace gases because only small amounts of them are present.

Question: What **four gases** make up **almost 100 percent of dry air?**

Answer Strategy: **In the Book: Think and Search**

The question uses words that do not appear in the text, and the answer to the question is distributed throughout the paragraph. Students must think about the question and then search the paragraph for the answer. This is another example of a literal question and answer; it is the Comprehension level of Bloom's taxonomy. This exercise is appropriate for intermediate-level students and for beginners who are paired with an English-speaking student.

In My Head If the question cannot be answered simply by reading the text but requires the student to use higher-order thinking skills, the student must use one of two In My Head strategies to formulate the answer.

1. **Author and You** The answer is not spelled out in the selection, although the text does provide clues. Students must use information from the text, combined with critical thinking skills, to draw conclusions, make inferences or predictions, or make generalizations in order to answer the question.

In My Head: Author and You Model

> **Sample Text**
> As you walk home from school, the air is warm and still. The sky is full of thick, **dark clouds.** In the distance you see a **bright flash.** A few seconds later, you hear a **crack of thunder.**

Question: What will happen **next?**

Answer Strategy: **In My Head: Author and You**

The answer is not stated explicitly in the text. Students must use information from the text together with their own experiences to make the prediction.

Information: dark clouds, bright flash, crack of thunder

Experience: Those things mean it is about to storm.

Prediction: It will start to rain.

This is an example of an analytical question; it combines the Analysis and Synthesis levels of Bloom's taxonomy. This exercise is appropriate for intermediate and advanced students, although you will need to model orally and visually how to arrive at the prediction. Beginners should be exposed to this strategy but will not have the English language skills to complete this exercise (even though they possess the necessary higher-order thinking skills and could complete the exercise in their native language).

2. **On My Own** As in the Author and You strategy, the answer is not spelled out in the selection. Students use their own past experiences and prior knowledge to answer the question. However, unlike the Author and You strategy, the student's answers do not depend on the position of the author; that is, the answers are opinions. Using the On My Own strategy, there is no right or wrong answer.

In My Head: On My Own Model

Sample Text

As you walk home from school, the air is warm and still. The sky is full of thick, dark clouds. In the distance you see a bright flash. A few seconds later, you hear a crack of thunder.

Question: What do you like to do when it is raining outside?

Answer Strategy: **In My Head: On My Own**

Because their answer is an opinion, the student can answer this question without even reading the text. This is an example of an analytical question; it is at the application level of Bloom's taxonomy. This exercise is appropriate for high-intermediate and advanced levels, but students at all levels can benefit from this type of questioning. Beginning-level students should be exposed to this type of questioning, but the teacher needs to realize that the students' limited vocabulary and writing expertise will prevent them from writing or explaining their answer. Remember that while all

English Language Learners have the ability to do higher-order thinking, they may not be able to articulate their thoughts because of their limited language skills. Try having these students answer orally, with the help of an English-proficient partner. Answering On My Own questions can be very enriching for English Language Learners because it allows them to use higher-order thinking skills while developing their English vocabulary.

KWL Chart

A KWL chart (shown below and in Transparency 8) is a three-part chart that asks students to state what they already *know* about a topic, what they *want* to find out, and then what they have *learned* after reading about the topic. In short, the chart provides the student with a visual self-assessment of their knowledge about a particular topic before and after instruction. Just as important, the chart tells the teacher how much background knowledge students have about the topic, what students think is important to know about the topic, and students' level of comprehension after reading. The teacher will use this information to tailor his or her lessons accordingly and to reteach, if necessary.

This strategy will be most effective for ELL students if you complete the chart as a class and record their responses on a class KWL chart at the front of the room. That way students can share information, hear language spoken, and see the connection between the pronunciation of words and their written symbols.

Use Transparency 8 for your KWL chart. Have students draw the same chart on a sheet of paper. They may want to place the chart on their papers sideways, and place each head at the top of the columns formed.

What Do I KNOW?
What Do I WANT to Know?
What Have I LEARNED?

Brainstorm What You Already Know Ask students to brainstorm what they already know about the given subject. Encourage all students to participate. If necessary, pair English Language Learners with English speakers to accommodate students at all language levels. For example, allow beginning-level ELL students to answer in their native language and, with the help of another student, to translate their answer into English. Usually, they will answer with words or phrases, rather than in complete sentences.

Write all the information from the brainstorming session in the top box of the class KWL chart. Have students help you categorize the information. Then have students record their individual responses in the top box of their KWL chart.

Think About What You Want to Know Before they begin reading, ask students what they want to find out in the selection. Encourage them to respond in the form of a question (for example, What are the phases of the moon?). Record their questions in the middle box of the class chart. Then have students write the questions that are important to them in the middle box of their own KWL charts.

Review What You Have Learned After reading, have students fill in the "What have I LEARNED?" box of their KWL chart. Use the questions from the "What do I WANT to know?" section to guide the discussion.

Think-Pair-Share Strategy

English Language Learners learn discussion techniques in this follow-up comprehension activity. Keep in mind that the English language proficiency level of the students will impact the depth of discussion. In addition, the selection students read may have to be modified to allow for their language level and writing expertise. It is best to pair students for this exercise. To get the most benefit from this strategy, have the Word Wall in place for students' reference and allow them to use their student-developed science glossaries.

1. Have students read a selection you have chosen from the text, such as "Exploring the Use of Acids."

2. Suggest a topic from the selection, for example, "Uses of Acids."

3. Have students work in pairs and write down what they have learned about the topic. Allow them to reread the selection for clarification if necessary.

4. Ask each pair of students to share their responses with the class. Record students' responses on an overhead, on chart paper, or on the chalkboard.

5. Conclude the activity with a class discussion in which students evaluate the responses, highlighting important points and eliminating inappropriate responses. Refer to the illustrations in the book to lend additional support to the evaluation process.

Graphic Organizers

A graphic organizer is a visual representation of knowledge organized into patterns. Graphic organizers are valuable teaching tools because they get students actively involved in learning and help them develop their critical and creative thinking skills. Constructing a graphic organizer requires the student to acknowledge, evaluate, understand, and restate information in a meaningful, systematic way. You might say that a graphic organizer is really a visual representation of the way our brains process and store information.

Graphic organizers are appropriate for all students in all content areas, but they are especially helpful to the English Language Learner. They help the ELL student focus on what is important, and by highlighting key vocabulary and concepts, they help the student remember it. Graphic organizers can also be used as alternative assessment tools. If each student constructs a graphic organizer before instruction, you can see what the student already knows about a topic. After instruction, a graphic organizer can tell you how well the student understands what he or she has been taught.

The rewards of using graphic organizers are many. They include the following:

- Students, in general, have a better attitude toward learning.

- Students have a better understanding and better retention of the material.

- Students' socialization skills improve. They learn to negotiate, evaluate, and work together, even though some members of the group may not be English proficient.

- Students' questioning ability improves as they look for meaning in the material presented.

- Students come to understand that there are different ways of representing knowledge and that how we organize information is influenced by culture, language, personality, and prior knowledge.

How to Use Graphic Organizers

Graphic organizers are more effective for the English Language Learner if they are taught using the following instructional approach:

1. Explain the purpose of graphic organizers.

2. Choose a graphic organizer that is appropriate for the language level of your students and the nature of the information to be organized. You may have to modify the graphic organizer to meet the language needs of your students.

3. Demonstrate how to organize information in the graphic organizer before providing guided or independent practice.

4. Give students an opportunity to demonstrate understanding by designing their own graphic organizer based on the material studied. You can have students work in groups, in pairs, or individually, depending on their language level.

5. Post the student-designed graphic organizers. Students can refer to them as they work on future assignments.

6. To enhance the English Language Learner's understanding of a graphic organizer, you may want to do one or more of the following:

   - Provide illustrations of the information in the graphic organizer, followed by descriptive words about the illustrations.

   - Use color-coding for main concepts or for the steps in a process.

   - For variety, draw graphic organizers on the chalkboard, on an overhead, on chart paper, or on a mural.

Types of Graphic Organizers

There are two basic types of graphic organizers; the type you use with your English Language Learners will depend on the topic you are studying. Sequential graphic organizers, such as flow charts and cycle diagrams, show a sequence of events or the steps or stages of a process. Conceptual graphic organizers, such as concept circles and maps, cause/effect charts, compare/contrast charts, and Venn diagrams, show how concepts are related. The following section explains how to use these different types of graphic organizers with English Language Learners.

Flow Chart (Transparency 1)

A flow chart is used to show a sequence of events in chronological order or the steps or stages in a process. Determine the number of boxes needed for the flow chart based on the information being presented. For example, one concept may call for only three boxes, whereas another concept may call for six. Just make sure the length and complexity of the flow chart are aligned with the English proficiency levels of your students. When simple illustrations can clarify the process, have students include them in the appropriate boxes. You may also want to color-code the steps. The following example shows the sequence of events in respiration.

The Path of Air

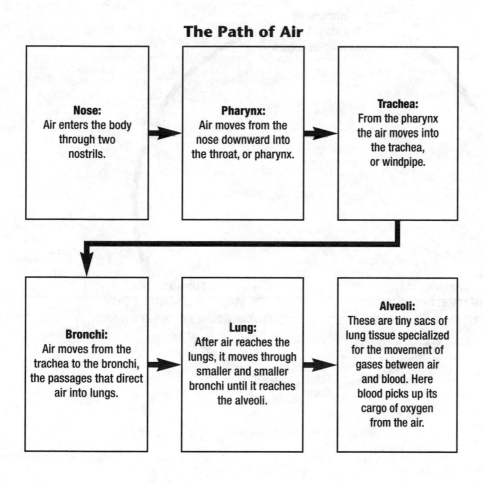

Cycle Diagram (Transparency 2)

A cycle diagram is similar to a flow chart in that it is used to show a sequence of events. In a cycle diagram, however, the sequence of events is continuous. Give students the opportunity to illustrate or build models of the steps to increase their comprehension of the cycle. The example of a cycle diagram below shows the process of cell division.

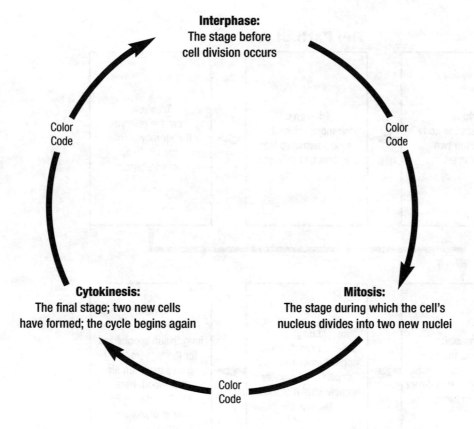

Interphase:
The stage before
cell division occurs

Color Code

Color Code

Mitosis:
The stage during which the cell's
nucleus divides into two new nuclei

Color Code

Cytokinesis:
The final stage; two new cells
have formed; the cycle begins again

Color Code

Concept Circle (Transparency 3)

A concept circle is a conceptual graphic organizer, which means it shows the relationship between a main concept or idea and supporting details. The main concept is written in a center circle, with the supporting details in boxes or circles around it. The supporting details are connected to the center circle with straight lines. To improve students' comprehension, have available illustrations of the supporting facts. In the concept circle below, for example, you might post an illustration of animals migrating when that particular subject is being taught.

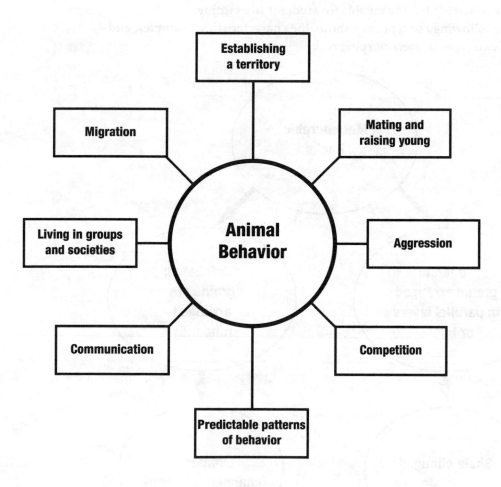

Modified Concept Map (Transparency 4)

A modified concept map or a hierarchical map is similar to a concept circle, but it is more detailed. The main concept is listed at the top, with successive levels of information underneath, each subordinate to the one above. Because of the hierarchical nature of concept maps, they can be quite complicated. You will need to decide how many subcategories to include in your organizer based on the language levels represented in your class. In general, to make the concept map more comprehensible for the English Language Learner, keep it simple; that is, place only the most important information on the map. You may also want to have illustrations or concrete objects available for students to examine.

The following concept map shows the characteristics, examples, and uses of two types of metamorphic rock.

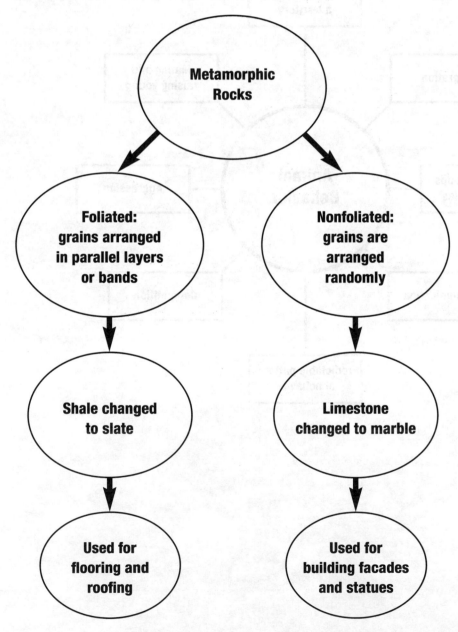

Cause/Effect Chart (Transparency 5)

A cause/effect chart is another way to show the relationship between concepts or facts. Its matrix format also makes it easy to compare items based on specific characteristics. A cause/effect chart will be more effective for the English Language Learner if it contains illustrations of the concepts presented.

Infectious Diseases

Cause (Pathogen)	Effect (Disease)
viruses	influenza
bacteria	strep throat
protists	malaria
fungi	athlete's foot

Compare/Contrast Chart (Transparency 6)

A compare/contrast chart is another type of conceptual graphic organizer. It is used for categorizing the similarities and differences between two items. To improve this graphic organizer's effectiveness, provide illustrations and icons, color-code important information, use a variety of materials to make the organizer, and design the organizer to reflect the language levels in the classroom.

Inclined Plane vs. Wedge

Similarities	Differences
Both are simple machines.	An inclined plane has one surface; a wedge has two.
Both make work easier.	An inclined plane does not move; a wedge does.
Both involve slanted surfaces.	A ramp is an example of an inclined plane; a knife is an example of a wedge.

Venn Diagram (Transparency 7)

A Venn diagram is a conceptual graphic organizer used to show the similarities and differences between two or more sets of items. The Venn diagram consists of two (or more) overlapping circles with an area of commonality in the middle. To enhance your ELL students' comprehension, use illustrations along with words, and color or shade the overlap section of the diagram to emphasize elements the items have in common. You might also list the common elements below the diagram.

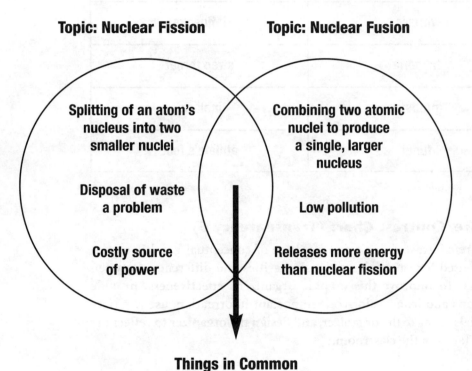

Topic: Nuclear Fission   **Topic: Nuclear Fusion**

Splitting of an atom's nucleus into two smaller nuclei

Disposal of waste a problem

Costly source of power

Combining two atomic nuclei to produce a single, larger nucleus

Low pollution

Releases more energy than nuclear fission

Things in Common

Both are nuclear reactions.

Both release energy.

Authentic/Alternative Assessment Strategies

Teachers in all content areas have struggled to find assessment strategies that will accurately measure the knowledge and abilities of their English Language Learners. Research has shown that without appropriate assessment strategies, ELL students may be graded inappropriately and placed in classes or programs in which they are destined to fail. Finding appropriate assessment practices is difficult because of wide variations in the language proficiency levels and prior school experiences of ELL students as well as in the levels of expertise of their content area teachers. Standardized tests alone do not give an accurate picture of the academic performance of these students. Therefore, teachers with English Language Learners in their classroom should consider authentic/alternative assessment strategies that contain the following components.

Open-Ended Questions

Having students write answers to open-ended questions not only gives them a chance to demonstrate their writing skills, but it assesses how well students understand what they have read, fosters higher-order thinking skills, and also reveals any misconceptions students may have about the content material.

Student-Created Products and Reports

Working individually, in pairs, or in groups, students produce a product or deliver a written or oral report to show comprehension of the assignment. Examples of student-created products include projects, experiments, and demonstrations. Reporting methods might include a written paper or an oral explanation accompanied by charts or other visuals, depending on the language proficiency of the student.

When using this method of assessment, assign tasks that are challenging, keeping in mind students' level of language proficiency. The tasks should be authentic—that is, activities found in the real world that are relevant to students' lives. It is also important that you model the reporting method by showing examples of what is required of students and explaining how the products will be assessed. The advantage of this form of assessment is that you can evaluate a student's level of comprehension at each step of the assignment.

Student Self-Evaluation

Let the students tell you what they already know and what they want to learn about the topic. Then let them tell you what they learned, how they learned it, and how they will use what they have learned. This can be accomplished by keeping a science journal, filling out a self-evaluation chart on a particular lesson, or designing a graphic organizer such as a KWL chart (discussed on page 23).

Student Assessment Scales

Student assessment scales are an effective way for students to assess not only what they have learned but what role they have played in completing a group assignment. This can be accomplished through simple questions on a student self-assessment page, for example: What did I contribute to the group in completing the assignment? How was I successful in completing the assignment? and What was one area of success?

For certain questions, you could have students assess themselves on a scale of 1–5 or 1–10. However, be aware of those students who assign themselves the very lowest number. Meet with them to discuss how they can improve their scores.

A variation of this is for the student to rate himself or herself while you rate the student. In most cases your scores will be similar. Consider it a "red flag"—especially for your English Language Learners—if the two scores vary widely.

Scientific Inquiry and English Language Learners

Scientific inquiry involves studying the natural world through objective analysis. It includes processes such as making observations, posing questions, identifying problems, formulating hypotheses, testing hypotheses through controlled experiments, collecting and interpreting data, and drawing conclusions on the basis of data. English Language Learners may have difficulty with methods of scientific inquiry partly because of their limited science background but also because of their lack of oral English proficiency, undeveloped English composition skills, and inexperience using higher-level thinking skills, such as analyzing and inferring, in English. The strategies suggested below will enable you to help your ELL students use scientific processes.

Posing Questions and Identifying Problems

In order to pose scientific questions or identify problems, students will need some background knowledge of the topic. Begin by brainstorming with students to determine how much they know about the topic. Use a graphic organizer such as a KWL chart or a modified concept map for the benefit of your English Language Learners. (These organizers are explained in detail on pages 23 and 30.)

It's possible that your ELL students will not have adequate background knowledge to identify a problem. Give all students a chance to build or reinforce background knowledge by researching the topic. Be sure to provide research materials, such as magazines and trade and reference books.

Following the brainstorming and research sessions, lead students to identify a problem by asking them a series of questions about it. Make sure that your questions can be understood by students at all levels of English proficiency. (See the Oral Language Proficiency Chart on page 9.) Be prepared to use visuals, such as pictures, charts, and even gestures, to make yourself understood.

Developing a Hypothesis

Once students have identified a problem, guide them to make a logical hypothesis based on their previous science experience and background knowledge of the topic. A hypothesis is a possible explanation or answer to a scientific question; it is a prediction that can be tested. To help students understand this, model some sample problems and hypotheses on chart paper or on the board. For example:

Question: Why does my puppy bark all night?

Hypothesis: It barks because it is hungry.

You may want to place students in cooperative groups when developing their own hypotheses.

Designing and Conducting an Experiment

Guide students through the process of making a written plan for their experiment. Again, you may want to have ELL students work in pairs or cooperative groups with English speakers. Give each pair or group a sheet of mural paper and have students record the steps of their experiment in both pictures and words. The design must include the following:

- A statement of the problem

- The steps of the experiment

- Illustrations or sketches of what the experimental setup will look like

- Student responsibilities while conducting the experiment

- A prediction of the results of the experiment

Collecting and Recording Data

Have students work in pairs or groups to collect and record data. Keep in mind, however, that English Language Learners at the same proficiency level should never be paired up for data collection. Instead, pair students who have writing expertise with students who use illustrations or symbols to express themselves. Data collection should then take place as follows: One student takes accurate notes on the observations while the other student adds illustrations or diagrams or arranges the data. You may need to explain to your ELL students how to organize the data they collect—for example, by using data tables, sketches, or written observations. The best way to do this is to model the data collection process.

Interpreting the Data

For the benefit of your English Language Learners, copy students' data on sheets of chart paper and post them on the wall. Then, using different-color markers to represent different categories of information, have students circle information they feel is important to the experiment. Discuss with students what type of visual representation would work best for the data, and if it is a graph, discuss which data sets will be the variables. Once students have completed their graphs, have them look for trends in the data, paying particular attention to data that do not fit the trend. Discuss whether the anomalous data should be discarded or should be used to adjust or replace the trend.

Drawing Conclusions

Begin by having students review the problem they identified or the question they posed. Next, have students make inferences about the problem based on the data they collected. Students must work cooperatively to come to a conclusion about the problem. Then have them compare their conclusion to their original hypothesis. Finally, discuss with students how their knowledge of or opinions about the topic have changed due to the results of the experiment.

Science Explorer and ELLs

Science Explorer is friendly to the English Language Learner because it addresses the affective, linguistic, and cognitive aspects of learning. The chart below summarizes how the pedagogy and features of each section help English Language Learners understand new concepts presented in a language that is unfamiliar to them. *Science Explorer* gives all students, regardless of language levels, the opportunity to use their imagination, to use skills such as observing, summarizing, and inferring, and to see that everyone can learn science and pursue a scientific career regardless of gender or ethnic background.

Discover	• Activities relevant to real life motivate students to learn both the content and the language. • Think It Over questions give opportunities for critical thinking.
Guide for Reading	• Important points are highlighted so students can look for them in the reading. • Reading Tip suggests activities to make the reading more meaningful.
Section Titles, Subsection Heads	• Titles help students understand what they will be reading and see the basic vocabulary before they begin reading. • Section titles and subsection heads outline the content presented.
Vocabulary Words	• Vocabulary is emphasized through the use of boldface words. • Each term is defined in easy-to-read terms, and often is connected to a visual. • The text allows students to infer the meaning of the vocabulary words through context clues.
Photographs, Diagrams, Charts, and Graphs	• Photos of real people representing diverse ethnic groups allow students to see themselves interacting with science concepts. • Diagrams, charts, and graphs organize information for visual interpretation. • Visuals and text are closely linked, giving students with less language proficiency a visual overview of concepts.
Checkpoint	• Ongoing comprehension checks let students know whether they understand key concepts.
Exploring	• Visual exploration of concepts provides access to students without higher-level language skills.
In Your Journal	• Writing about science concepts provides language stimulation and opportunities to translate concepts into the students' own words.
Section Reviews	• Ongoing assessment helps students know whether they have grasped the basic content and can use their higher-level critical thinking skills.
Skills Labs and Real World Labs	• Clear, step-by-step instructions allow students to follow modeled procedures and to work in small, incremental steps. • Labs allow students to reinforce new vocabulary and concepts by using manipulatives and laboratory equipment.

Sample Lesson: Life Science
The Muscular System

Preparing the Lesson

Assess Prior Knowledge

Use a three-column KWL chart (Transparency 8) with the three boxes labeled What Do I KNOW, What Do I WANT to Know, and What Have I LEARNED. Accept reasonable responses to What Do I KNOW. The students may give their response in their native language, by a gesture, or by working in pairs to develop a response in English. Beginning English Language Learners may find it difficult to give a response to What Do I WANT to Know because it requires higher-order thinking skills that are not yet developed in English. Be prepared with some responses and gestures to guide the students. After completing the first two boxes of the chart, keep the chart on display while the section is taught. After reading the section, students can return to the chart to respond to What Have I LEARNED. Including a visual of the topic on any student- or teacher-made chart will facilitate understanding.

Key Words

Develop a Word Wall (discussed on page 14) using the key terms *involuntary muscle, voluntary muscle, skeletal muscle, smooth muscle, cardiac muscle, tendon,* and *striated muscle.* Place the title "The Muscular System" at the top with the key terms under it. For each vocabulary word, include the definition and a visual that represents the word or connects to the word.

As you teach the lesson, add words that appear to confuse the English Language Learner. Make sure to highlight prefixes such as *in-* attached to *involuntary* so students will see how the definition of a root word is modified by a prefix. Remember to refer to the key terms during instruction and include them in any homework assignment. Encourage the students to refer to the Word Wall during guided or independent practice when they need help in understanding a vocabulary word. Allow students time to write key vocabulary words from a Word Wall in their science glossaries (discussed on page 12).

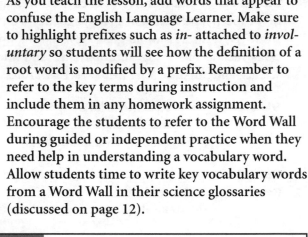

SECTION 3 The Muscular System

DISCOVER

How Do Muscles Work?

1. Grip a spring-type clothespin with the thumb and index finger of your writing hand. Squeeze the clothespin open and shut as quickly as possible for two minutes. Count how many times you can squeeze the clothespin before your muscles tire.

2. Rest for one minute. Then repeat Step 1.

Think It Over

Predicting What do you think would happen if you repeated Steps 1 and 2 with your other hand? Give a reason for your prediction. Then test your prediction.

GUIDE FOR READING

◆ What three types of muscles are found in the body?

◆ Why do skeletal muscles work in pairs?

Reading Tip Before you read, preview Figure 14. Predict the functions of skeletal, smooth, and cardiac muscle. After you read the section, look back at your predictions to see whether they were correct.

A rabbit becomes still when it senses danger. The rabbit sits so still that it doesn't seem to move a muscle. Could you sit without moving any muscles? If you tried to, you'd find that it is impossible to sit still for very long. Saliva builds up in your mouth. You swallow. You need to breathe. Your chest expands to let air in. All of these actions involve muscles.

There are about 600 muscles in your body. Muscles have many functions. For example, they keep your heart beating, pull your mouth into a smile, and move the bones of your skeleton.

Muscle Action

Some of your body's movements, such as smiling, are easy to control. Other movements, such as the beating of your heart, are impossible to control completely. That is because some muscles are not under your conscious control. Those muscles are called **involuntary muscles.** Involuntary muscles are responsible for activities such as breathing and digesting food.

The muscles that are under your control are called **voluntary muscles.** Smiling, turning a page in a book, and getting out of your chair when the bell rings are all actions controlled by voluntary muscles.

◀ A rabbit "frozen" in place

Discover

Begin by explaining what a clothespin is and how it is used. Then model the activity for students. Pair the students; have them complete the activity, and record their results. Allow students to talk and express their reactions in their native language during this time. Then have the students write and test their prediction for the questions in "Think It Over." Follow up with a discussion of the students' results.

Reading Tip

Guide the students to preview Figure 14. Have the students locate a cardiac muscle, a smooth muscle, and a skeletal muscle on their own body. From the locations of the muscles have students infer what each type of muscle does. They can then write

each prediction as a complete sentence on a strip of paper. Place these sentence strips on the visual of the appropriate muscle.

Reading the Lesson

Muscle Action

Before Reading Have students look at the picture of the rabbit "frozen" in place. Tell the students to "freeze." Have them sit "frozen" for one minute. After the minute ask students how they felt when they were "frozen." What actions did they continue to do and what actions did they not do when they were "frozen"?

During Reading Call attention to the terms *involuntary muscle* and *voluntary muscle*. Direct students' attention to the Word Wall where the words, definitions, and visuals of involuntary and voluntary muscles are shown. Use a T-chart with *Involuntary muscle* on one side and *Voluntary muscle* on the other side. Have students draw their own copies of this chart. Then have students read the subsection "Muscle Action" and write the attributes of involuntary muscles on the correct side of their T-chart. They should do the same with voluntary muscles.

After Reading Ask, "How do your answers connect to the rabbit frozen in place or you in a frozen position?" A discussion should follow, allowing translations to take place if needed by the English Language Learners.

Types of Muscles

Before Reading Read aloud the first sentence in the paragraph that identifies the three types of muscle tissue. Direct students' attention to the Word Wall where they will see the words, definitions, and visuals of the types of muscle tissue. Have the students look ahead and preview the headings "Skeletal Muscle," "Smooth

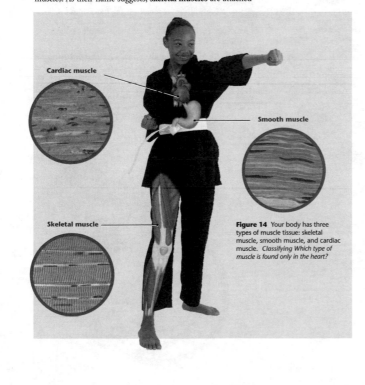

Types of Muscles

Your body has three types of muscle tissue—skeletal muscle, smooth muscle, and cardiac muscle. In Figure 14, you see a magnified view of each type of muscle in the body. Both skeletal and smooth muscles are found in many places in the body. Cardiac muscle is found only in the heart. Each muscle type performs specific functions in the body.

Skeletal Muscle Every time you type on a computer keyboard, shoot a basketball, or walk across a room, you are using skeletal muscles. As their name suggests, **skeletal muscles** are attached

Cardiac muscle

Smooth muscle

Skeletal muscle

Figure 14 Your body has three types of muscle tissue: skeletal muscle, smooth muscle, and cardiac muscle. *Classifying Which type of muscle is found only in the heart?*

Muscle," and "Cardiac Muscle" as well as any other vocabulary word in bold letters, such as *tendon*.

During Reading Place students into groups integrated by language level. Assign each group one of the three types of muscles. Each group should develop its own definition of the assigned muscle, illustrate the description, and list its characteristics, including whether the muscle is involuntary or voluntary.

After Reading After the students complete the exercise, check for comprehension by having the students report, group by group, on their type of muscle. Display the group work if possible.

Checkpoint

Ask which group had the muscle that reacts and tires quickly. Then ask why the other two muscles do not tire easily. Put these responses on sentence strips or on the board so students can see language written as well as hear it spoken.

Try This

Pair each English Language Learner with a student who has a high level of English proficiency or with a native English speaker. Model the activity using the "think aloud" strategy, emphasizing what is meant by *parallel*, *hairpin*, *legs of the hairpin*, *head of the hairpin*. With a "think aloud" strategy, the teacher verbalizes all the steps of the activity as well as the definitions of materials, so that students understand the thinking processes involved. This strategy facilitates vocabulary and language development as well as modeling for students what they will be doing.

Be prepared to help students as pairs of students work on the activity. Watch for understanding of the task by the English Language Learners.

Let students discuss with one another the answer to the inference question. Allow one or two students to give the answer to the whole class. Check with the English Language Learners to be sure they understand.

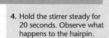

Get a Grip

ACTIVITY

Are skeletal muscles at work when you're not moving? Try this activity and see.

1. Hold a stirrer in front of you, parallel to a table top. Do not touch the table.

2. Have a partner place a hairpin on the stirrer.

3. Raise the stirrer until the "legs" of the hairpin just touch the table. The "head" of the hairpin should rest on the stirrer, as you see in the photo.

4. Hold the stirrer steady for 20 seconds. Observe what happens to the hairpin.

5. Grip the stirrer tighter and repeat Step 4. Observe what happens.

Inferring Based on your observations, are the skeletal muscles in your hand at work when you hold your hand still? Explain.

to the bones of your skeleton. These muscles provide the force that moves your bones. At each end of a skeletal muscle is a tendon. A **tendon** is a strong connective tissue that attaches muscle to bone. As you can see in Figure 14, skeletal muscle cells appear banded, or striated (STRY ay tid). For this reason, skeletal muscle is sometimes called striated muscle.

Because you have conscious control of skeletal muscles, they are classified as voluntary muscles. One characteristic of skeletal muscles is that they react very quickly. You can see an example of just how quickly skeletal muscle reacts by watching a swim meet. Immediately after the starting gun sounds, a swimmer's leg muscles quickly push the swimmer off the block into the pool. However, another characteristic of skeletal muscles is that they tire quickly. By the end of the race, the swimmer's muscles are tired and need a rest.

Smooth Muscle The inside of many internal organs of the body, such as the walls of the stomach and blood vessels, contain smooth muscles. **Smooth muscles** are involuntary muscles. They work automatically to control many types of movements inside your body, such as those involved in the process of digestion. For example, as the smooth muscles of your stomach contract, they produce a churning action. The churning mixes the food with chemicals produced by your stomach. This action and these chemicals help to digest the food.

Muscles at Work

Have the students "make a muscle." As they are doing this, explain to the students what is happening to the muscle. Direct students' attention to Figure 15. Point to the noted parts on your arm and have students do the same to their arms. Ask, "What happens to each muscle to straighten the arm?" Then allow time for the students to bend and straighten the knee joint to see the connectivity between the functions of muscles.

Taking Care of Your Skeletal Muscles

Direct the students' attention to Figure 16. Ask, "What is this person doing? Why is it important that she does this?" Find out from students how they warm up before exercising. Choose the most important sentence in each of the three paragraphs and write each on the board or overhead. Possible choices are the following.

- **Exercise is important for maintaining both muscular strength and flexibility.**
- **Some of the same precautions that help prevent bone and joint injuries can also help prevent muscle injuries.**
- **Sometimes, despite taking proper precautions, muscles can become injured.**

Emphasize each important sentence to the students, having them read the paragraph looking for evidence to support the statement. List those reasons on the board under the sentence. Be sure that all students have the opportunity to participate. Ask for a response from the English Language Learners even if they do not volunteer. However, non-English speakers or newcomers should not be forced to speak. If possible, however, pair them with someone who speaks their native language and have the non-English speaker give a response that the native speaker can convey to you. Be sure that you then look at the non-English speaker and acknowledge the answer. This practice raises the self-esteem and comfort level for the non-English speaker in the classroom, which will facilitate language development.

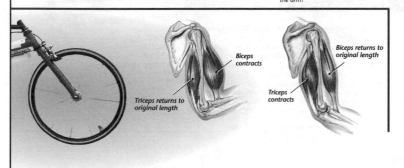

Unlike skeletal muscles, smooth muscle cells are not striated. Smooth muscles behave differently than skeletal muscles, too. Smooth muscles react more slowly and tire more slowly.

Cardiac Muscle The tissue called **cardiac muscle** has characteristics in common with both smooth and skeletal muscles. Like smooth muscle, cardiac muscle is involuntary. Like skeletal muscle, cardiac muscle cells are striated. However, unlike skeletal muscle, cardiac muscle does not get tired. It can contract repeatedly. You call those repeated contractions heartbeats.

Checkpoint Which type of muscle reacts and tires quickly?

Muscles at Work

Has anyone ever asked you to "make a muscle"? If so, you probably tightened your fist, bent your arm at the elbow, and made the muscles in your upper arm bulge. Like other skeletal muscles, the muscles in your arm do their work by contracting, or becoming shorter and thicker. Muscle cells contract when they receive messages from the nervous system. **Because muscle cells can only contract, not extend, skeletal muscles must work in pairs. While one muscle contracts, the other muscle in the pair returns to its original length.**

Figure 15 shows the muscle action involved in bending the arm at the elbow. First, the biceps muscle on the front of the upper arm contracts to bend the elbow, lifting the forearm and hand. As the biceps contracts, the triceps on the back of the upper arm returns to its original length. Then to straighten the elbow, the triceps muscle contracts. As the triceps contracts to extend the arm, the biceps returns to its original length. Another example of muscles that work in pairs are those in your thigh that bend and straighten the knee joint.

Figure 15 Because muscles can only contract, or shorten, they must work in pairs. To bend the arm at the elbow, the biceps contracts while the triceps returns to its original length. *Interpreting Diagrams What happens to each muscle to straighten the arm?*

Biceps contracts

Triceps returns to original length

Biceps returns to original length

Triceps contracts

Assessing the Lesson

Section 3 Review

English Language Learners need to be assessed at their language ability. Allow illustrations, simple sentences, group work, experiments, and collaborative work when assessing ELL students. Allow use of student glossaries, Word Walls, notes, or student-developed graphics to demonstrate comprehension. Most important, assess English Language Learners at their language level to gain a true understanding of their comprehension of the content.

Question 1 All levels of English Language Learners should be able to identify the three types of muscles and where they are found. Beginning-level students can show their knowledge through illustrations and labeling. Refer to Figure 14 if they need a model for comprehension. Allow students to use any material completed in the classroom to design a response.

Question 2 Allow English Language Learners, particularly those at the beginning level, to physically show they understand how the muscles in the arm work. Students at other levels of language may refer to Figure 15 and write and illustrate answers. Remember that some students may have oral language but little

expertise in writing, which you should take into consideration when assessing responses.

Question 3 English Language Learners will benefit from drawing a T-chart to answer this question. Beginning English Language Learners will need to refer to previous work for vocabulary. Students at all other levels should be able to respond to this question.

Question 4, Thinking Critically Have English Language Learners work in groups to respond to this question. Provide visuals of the situation, review the vocabulary word *tendon*, and allow for discussion among the group members to decide upon a prediction. Assess responses through oral group responses, written responses from the group, and informal observation as discussions are taking place.

Taking Care of Your Skeletal Muscles

INTEGRATING HEALTH Exercise is important for maintaining both muscular strength and flexibility. Exercise makes individual muscle cells grow wider. This, in turn, causes the whole muscle to become thicker. The thicker a muscle is, the stronger the muscle is. When you stretch and warm up thoroughly, your muscles become more flexible. This helps prepare your muscles for the work involved in exercising or playing.

Figure 16 When you warm up before exercising, you increase the flexibility of your muscles.

Like your bones and joints, your skeletal muscles are subject to injuries. Some of the same precautions that help prevent bone and joint injuries can also help prevent muscle injuries. For example, warming up increases the flexibility of joints as well as muscles. In addition, using proper safety equipment can protect all of your tissues, including muscles and tendons.

Sometimes, despite taking proper precautions, muscles can become injured. A muscle strain, or a pulled muscle, can occur when muscles are overworked or overstretched. Tendons can also be overstretched or partially torn. After a long period of exercise, a skeletal muscle can cramp. When a muscle cramps, the entire muscle contracts strongly and stays contracted. If you injure a muscle or tendon, it is important to follow medical instructions and to rest the injured area until it heals.

 Section 3 Review

1. Name the three types of muscle tissue. Where is each type found?
2. Describe how the muscles in your upper arm work together to bend and straighten your arm.
3. How do voluntary and involuntary muscles differ? Give an example of each type of muscle.
4. **Thinking Critically Predicting** The muscles that move your fingers are attached to the bones in your fingers by long tendons. Suppose one of the tendons in a person's index finger were cut all the way through. How would this injury affect the person's ability to move his or her index finger? Explain.

Check Your Progress
CHAPTER PROJECT
You should now be assembling your working model. Be sure that you include the muscles involved in the movement you are modeling. Also, remember that your model must show how muscle contractions produce the chosen movement. (*Hint:* After you have assembled your model, do a final check to be sure it functions the way it should.)

Skills Lab

A Look Beneath the Skin

Explain the expectations of the lab before beginning. Make sure students understand that they will be learning about their own skeletal muscles by observing the "arm" or wing muscles of a chicken. Beginning English Language Learners need to hear the word *wing* in addition to the word *arm*.

Problem

Review characteristics of skeletal muscles and how they work. If necessary for comprehension, review charts, graphs, illustrations, and vocabulary.

Procedure

Pair the English Language Learner with someone who is at a higher language level and is willing to help the English Language Learner understand the procedure. Model every step of the procedure and seat the English Language Learners where they can have eye contact with you during the procedure. This practice facilitates comprehension for the students.

Analyze and Conclude

Have the English Language Learners diagram their responses to questions 1 and 2. Allow plenty of time, because the students may not comprehend beyond what they see. It may be difficult for them to explain how the chicken wing moves at the elbow and compare that to how their elbow moves. Their levels of response will depend on their levels of English. Accept literal answers and diagrams from the nonproficient speakers.

Advanced-level and transitional students will be able to write about the higher-order thinking that is required. Be sure to discuss the answers to these questions, because all English Language Learners need to hear the responses even though their language levels may differ. All groups should be able to classify the muscles they are observing.

Think About It

Have on hand an example of a well-drawn diagram and one that is not completed accurately. Have the class discuss and understand why it is important to be accurate when recording observations with diagrams.

More to Explore

Challenge students to use the procedures from this skills lab to compare a chicken leg to a human leg. Students can do this activity at home and describe their results in class. Remind the students to be accurate in their observations and diagrams.

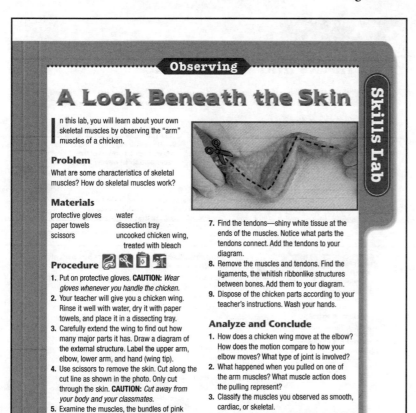

Observing

A Look Beneath the Skin

Skills Lab

In this lab, you will learn about your own skeletal muscles by observing the "arm" muscles of a chicken.

Problem
What are some characteristics of skeletal muscles? How do skeletal muscles work?

Materials
protective gloves
paper towels
scissors
water
dissection tray
uncooked chicken wing, treated with bleach

Procedure
1. Put on protective gloves. **CAUTION:** *Wear gloves whenever you handle the chicken.*
2. Your teacher will give you a chicken wing. Rinse it well with water, dry it with paper towels, and place it in a dissecting tray.
3. Carefully extend the wing to find out how many major parts it has. Draw a diagram of the external structure. Label the upper arm, elbow, lower arm, and hand (wing tip).
4. Use scissors to remove the skin. Cut along the cut line as shown in the photo. Only cut through the skin. **CAUTION:** *Cut away from your body and your classmates.*
5. Examine the muscles, the bundles of pink tissue around the bones. Find the two groups of muscles in the upper arm. Hold the arm down at the shoulder, and alternately pull on each muscle group. Observe what happens.
6. Find the two groups of muscles in the lower arm. Hold down the arm at the elbow, and alternately pull on each muscle group. Then make a diagram of the wing's muscles.
7. Find the tendons—shiny white tissue at the ends of the muscles. Notice what parts the tendons connect. Add the tendons to your diagram.
8. Remove the muscles and tendons. Find the ligaments, the whitish ribbonlike structures between bones. Add them to your diagram.
9. Dispose of the chicken parts according to your teacher's instructions. Wash your hands.

Analyze and Conclude
1. How does a chicken wing move at the elbow? How does the motion compare to how your elbow moves? What type of joint is involved?
2. What happened when you pulled on one of the arm muscles? What muscle action does the pulling represent?
3. Classify the muscles you observed as smooth, cardiac, or skeletal.
4. **Think About It** Why is it valuable to record your observations with accurate diagrams?

More to Explore
Use the procedures from this lab to examine an uncooked chicken thigh and leg. Compare how the chicken leg and a human leg move.

Sample Lesson: Earth Science
Rocks and Weathering

Preparing the Lesson

Assess Prior Knowledge

Ask students if anyone has been hiking or *tramping* (as some English Language Learners call it) in the mountains. If so, give them the opportunity to answer and volunteer information, as conversation fosters language development. Display a map of the United States with the Appalachian Mountains outlined in red and the Sierra Nevada outlined in blue to show their geographic locations. Discuss the locations and refer the students to Figure 1. Explain that one picture is of the Sierra Nevada and the other is of the Appalachian Mountains. Discuss how the two mountain ranges look different as well as how they are similar.

Key Terms

Prepare a Word Wall (discussed on page 14) for this section. Post the key terms *(weathering, erosion, mechanical weathering, ice wedging, chemical weathering, permeable)*, and any other words the students might stumble on, along with the definitions and visuals that will assist in comprehension. Since the title of this section can highlight how adding *–ing* changes the meaning of a word, underline the *–ing* in *weathering*. At some point when using the Word Wall, bring the *–ing* into the conversation and explain how the meaning of *weather* changes when it becomes *weathering*.

Discover

Pair students to allow for language exchange. Before the students complete the activity, model it for them. To enhance understanding of the whole tablet representing a solid rock and the ground-up tablet representing rock fragments, display a solid rock and rock fragments. English Language Learners at all language levels can either write, say, or point to the tablet that dissolved the fastest. When asking questions orally about the implications of the activity, frame the questions in simple sentences for the beginning and intermediate speakers so they may answer with one- or two-word responses or simple sentences. Students at other levels may answer with a longer narrative in English that reflects more complex thoughts.

Rocks and Weathering

DISCOVER

How Fast Can It Fizz?

1. Place a fizzing antacid tablet in a small beaker. Then grind up a second tablet and place it in another beaker. The whole tablet is a model of solid rock. The ground-up tablet is a model of rock fragments.

2. Add 100 mL of warm water to the beaker containing the whole tablet. Then stir with a stirring rod until the tablet dissolves completely. Use a stopwatch to time how long it takes.

3. Add 100 mL of warm water to the beaker containing the ground-up tablet. Then stir until all of the ground-up tablet dissolves. Time how long it takes.

Think It Over

Inferring Which dissolved faster, the whole antacid tablet or the ground-up tablet? What difference between the two affected how long it took them to dissolve?

GUIDE FOR READING

◆ What causes mechanical weathering?

◆ What causes chemical weathering?

◆ What determines how fast weathering occurs?

Reading Tip As you read, use the headings to make an outline about weathering.

Imagine a hike that lasts for months and covers hundreds of kilometers. Each year, many hikers go on such treks. They hike trails that run the length of America's great mountain ranges. For example, the John Muir Trail follows the Sierra Nevada mountains. The Sierras extend about 640 kilometers along the eastern side of California. In the east, the Appalachian Trail follows the Appalachian Mountains. The Appalachians stretch more than 2,000 kilometers from Alabama to Maine.

The two trails cross very different landscapes. The Sierras are rocky and steep, with many peaks rising 3,000 meters above sea level. The Appalachians are more rounded and gently sloping, and are covered with soil and plants. The highest peaks in the Appalachians are less than half the elevation of the highest peaks in the Sierras. Which mountain range do you think is older? The Appalachians formed more than 250 million years ago. The Sierras formed only within the last 10 million years. The forces that wear down rock on Earth's surface have had much longer to grind down the Appalachians.

The Effects of Weathering

The process of mountain building thrusts rock up to the Earth's surface. There, the rock becomes exposed to weathering. **Weathering** is the process that breaks down rock and other substances at Earth's surface. Heat, cold, water, and ice all contribute to weathering. So do the oxygen and carbon dioxide in the atmosphere. Repeated freezing

---

Reading Tip

Have each student draw a Venn diagram (Transparency 7) as you model how to do it. In one circle, instruct students to write the properties of the Appalachian Mountains and in the other circle have them write the properties of the Sierra Nevada. Tell students to put the commonalities of the two mountain ranges in the common area of the Venn diagram. After students complete the Venn diagram, elicit responses from the students as to what they included and where they put the terms. Discuss why they put the responses where they did. Then go to a higher level of questions and ask, "What are the implications about our country based on what you found out about the mountains?" Write the responses on the Venn diagram transparency. Keep the Venn diagram displayed as a reference for students and as a teaching tool.

Reading the Lesson

The Effects of Weathering

Before Reading In order for students to organize and understand this section, have them form a review outline. Have students complete their outline individually as you model and facilitate the process. Make the outline in the form of a concept map, with the center being *Rocks and Weathering*. Use the topics highlighted in green in the text to make the spokes of the concept map. As students design and complete their concept maps, call attention to the vocabulary words on the Word Wall and in the concept map so students can start making the correlation between the vocabulary and the text.

Bring the word *weathering* to the students' attention. Have students pronounce the word with you. Then have students read the definition and observe a visual on the Word Wall. Follow the same procedure with the word *erosion*.

Have students write out the following guide questions. To help the students understand the text of each question, display a visual that shows the causes and effects of weathering.

1. What is weathering?
2. What causes or contributes to weathering?
3. What are some examples of weathering?

and thawing, for example, can crack rock apart into smaller pieces. Rainwater can dissolve minerals that bind rock together. You don't need to go to the mountains to see examples of weathering. The forces that wear down mountains also cause bicycles to rust, paint to peel, sidewalks to crack, and potholes to form.

The forces of weathering break rocks into smaller and smaller pieces. Then the forces of erosion carry the pieces away. **Erosion** (ee ROH zhun) is the movement of rock particles by wind, water, ice, or gravity. Weathering and erosion work together continuously to wear down and carry away the rocks at Earth's surface.

There are two kinds of weathering: mechanical weathering and chemical weathering. Both types of weathering act slowly, but over time they break down even the biggest, hardest rocks.

✔ *Checkpoint* What is the difference between weathering and erosion?

Figure 1 The jagged, rocky peaks of the Sierra Nevadas (left) show that the mountains are young. The more gently sloping Appalachians (right) have been exposed to weathering for 250 million years.

Mechanical Weathering

If you hit a rock hard enough with a hammer, the rock will break into pieces. Some forces of weathering can also break rock into pieces. The type of weathering in which rock is physically broken into smaller pieces is called **mechanical weathering.** These smaller pieces of rock have the same composition as the rock they came from. If you have seen rocks that are cracked or peeling in layers, then you have seen rocks that are undergoing mechanical weathering.

Mechanical weathering breaks rock into pieces by freezing and thawing, release of pressure, growth of plants, actions of animals, and abrasion. The term **abrasion** (uh BRAY zhun) refers to the grinding away of rock by rock particles carried by water, ice, wind, or gravity. Mechanical weathering works slowly. But over very long periods of time, it does more than wear down rocks. Mechanical weathering eventually wears away whole mountains.

During Reading As the students read the first paragraph of this section have them answer the guide questions. If English Language Learners can read the text but not yet write a response in English, give choices, depending upon the language level of the students, such as illustrate only, illustrate and write, or write only. As students read the second paragraph, have them list the properties of erosion.

After Reading During the discussion of student responses to the guide questions, connect the visuals with their responses. Invite students to share the properties of erosion. Check students' comprehension of erosion and weathering by having them illustrate the difference between the two concepts. Depending upon the language level of the students, you may wish to allow them to use visuals to help them get started. Display their completed illustrations.

Mechanical Weathering

Before Reading Call attention to the Word Wall and point out the terms *mechanical weathering*, *abrasion*, and *ice wedging* and their definitions along with visuals of the results of mechanical weathering. Have students read the words and definitions aloud chorally. Invite students to look at the photos in the feature to see how mechanical weathering affects rocks on the earth's surface.

During Reading Have students derive their own definition of mechanical weathering based on the paragraphs and visuals. Help them to begin the definition by writing the following on the board: "Mechanical weathering breaks rocks into pieces by——————." Let students write in the remainder of the definition as they read the text. Allow for differences in vocabulary depending upon the language expertise of the student.

After Reading Let each student choose one of the forces of mechanical weathering shown in the text and illustrate it. Use these and other illustrations from this section as part of a "mini-science museum" in the room. Encourage students to take the time to look at each other's work. After a time rotate with new material.

INTEGRATING PHYSICS In cool climates, the most important force of mechanical weathering is freezing and thawing of water. Water seeps into cracks in rocks and then freezes when the temperature drops. Water expands when it freezes. Ice therefore acts like a wedge, a simple machine that forces things apart. Wedges of ice in rocks widen and deepen cracks. This process is called **ice wedging**. When the ice melts, the water seeps deeper into the cracks. With repeated freezing and thawing, the cracks slowly expand until pieces of rock break off. *Exploring the Forces of Mechanical Weathering* shows how this process weathers rock.

Checkpoint How does ice wedging weather rock?

EXPLORING the Forces of Mechanical Weathering

Mechanical weathering affects all the rock on Earth's surface. Given enough time, mechanical weathering can break down a massive mountain into tiny particles of sand.

Release of Pressure
As erosion removes material from the surface of a mass of rock, pressure on the rock below is reduced. This release of pressure causes the outside of the rock to crack and flake off like the layers of an onion.

Freezing and Thawing
When water freezes in a crack in a rock, it expands and makes the crack bigger. The process of ice wedging also widens cracks in sidewalks and causes potholes in streets.

Chemical Weathering

Before Reading To introduce chemical weathering, have students look at the Word Wall to see the term, its definition, and a visual. Have the students read the description in the text. Ask them to list the agents of chemical weathering.

During Reading Prepare a graphic organizer on the board or chart paper using *Chemical Weathering* as the title. Cooperatively group the students and assign each group an agent of chemical weathering. Instruct the groups to come up with a sentence or two that best describes what their agent is as they read about the agents in the text.

After Reading Tell the groups to put their responses on sentence strips and place them under the heading *Chemical Weathering*. Lead a discussion to clarify comprehension of this term. Guide students to infer that chemical weathering produces rock particles that have a different mineral make-up from the original rock and that each rock is made up of one or more minerals.

Chemical Weathering

In addition to mechanical weathering, another type of weathering attacks rock. **Chemical weathering** is the process that breaks down rock through chemical changes. **The agents of chemical weathering include water, oxygen, carbon dioxide, living organisms, and acid rain.**

Chemical weathering produces rock particles that have a different mineral makeup from the rock they came from. Each rock is made up of one or more minerals. For example, granite is made up of several minerals, including feldspar, quartz, and mica. But chemical weathering of granite eventually changes the feldspar minerals to clay minerals.

Plant Growth
Roots of trees and other plants enter cracks in rocks. As the roots grow, they force the cracks farther apart. Over time, the roots of even small plants can pry apart cracked rocks.

Abrasion
Sand and other rock particles that are carried by wind, water, or ice can wear away exposed rock surfaces like sandpaper on wood. Wind-driven sand helped shape the rocks shown here.

Animal Actions
Animals that burrow in the ground—including moles, gophers, prairie dogs, and some insects—loosen and break apart rocks in the soil.

Guide students to look at Figure 2. Invite them to predict how chemical and mechanical weathering work together. Then have them do the following experiment based on Figure 2.

a. Give each student a square of clay and a piece of string. Explain that the clay square represents a rock.

b. Demonstrate how to use the string to divide the clay into eight pieces as shown in the second illustration of Figure 2. Then have students divide their pieces.

c. Tell students to break each of the small clay squares into eight smaller squares so that their clay resembles the third illustration of Figure 2.

d. Challenge students to explain what is represented by this process and how chemical and mechanical weathering work together.

Try This Activity—Rusting Away

Have students work in pairs. Instruct them to record their daily observations of the steel wool on a simple chart or in a student notebook. Have teams work together to answer the questions with either illustrations or written predictions. Make sure the English Language Learners understand what steel wool is and how it is used. If necessary, demonstrate how to use it.

Rate of Weathering

Before Reading Have students focus their attention on the sentence in bold letters in the first paragraph. Invite them to explain what they think it means.

During Reading Assign half of the class to read the section *Type of Rock* and answer the following questions. Make sure there are about the same number of ELLs in each half.

1. What is the definition of *permeable*?
2. What determines how fast a rock weathers?
3. Why does permeable rock weather chemically at a fast rate?

Assign the other half of the class to read the two paragraphs on climate and answer the following questions:

1. What does the word *climate* mean?
2. How do higher temperatures affect chemical reactions?
3. How are chemical and mechanical weathering affected by wet climates?

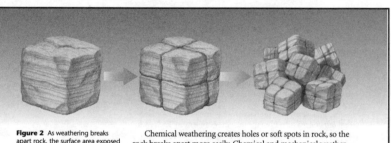

Figure 2 As weathering breaks apart rock, the surface area exposed to further weathering increases.

Chemical weathering creates holes or soft spots in rock, so the rock breaks apart more easily. Chemical and mechanical weathering often work together. As mechanical weathering breaks rock into pieces, more surface area becomes exposed to chemical weathering. The Discover activity in this section shows how increasing the surface area increases the rate of a chemical reaction.

Water Water is the most important agent of chemical weathering. Water weathers rock by dissolving it. When a rock or other substance dissolves in water, it mixes uniformly throughout the water to make a solution. Over time, many rocks will dissolve in water.

Oxygen The oxygen gas in air is an important cause of chemical weathering. If you have ever left a bicycle or metal tool outside in the rain, then you have seen how oxygen can weather iron. Iron combines with oxygen in the presence of water in a process called oxidation. The product of oxidation is rust. Rock that contains iron also oxidizes, or rusts. Rust makes rock soft and crumbly and gives it a red or brown color.

Carbon Dioxide Another gas found in air, carbon dioxide, also causes chemical weathering. Carbon dioxide becomes dissolved in rainwater and in water that sinks through air pockets in the soil. The result is a weak acid called carbonic acid. Carbonic acid easily weathers marble and limestone.

Living Organisms Imagine a seed landing on a rock face. As it sprouts, its roots push into cracks in the rock. As the plant's roots grow, they produce weak acids that slowly dissolve rock around the roots. Lichens—plantlike organisms that grow on rocks—also produce weak acids that chemically weather rock.

Acid Rain Over the past 150 years, people have been burning large amounts of coal, oil, and gas for energy. Burning these fuels can pollute the air with sulfur, carbon, and nitrogen compounds. Such compounds react chemically with the water vapor in clouds, forming acids. These acids mix with raindrops and fall as acid rain. Acid rain causes very rapid chemical weathering.

INTEGRATING ENVIRONMENTAL SCIENCE

TRY THIS

Rusting Away
Here's how you can observe weathering.

ACTIVITY

1. Moisten some steel wool and place it in a closed container so it will not dry out.

2. Observe the steel wool after a few days. What has happened to the steel wool?

3. Take a new piece of steel wool and squeeze it between your fingers. Remove the steel wool from the container and squeeze it between your fingers. What happens? Wash your hands when you have finished.

Predicting If you kept the steel wool moist for a longer time, what would eventually happen to it? How is the weathering of steel wool like the weathering of a rock?

After Reading Have each half of the class report its responses to the other group.

Guide the students to look at Figure 3. Explain what has happened to the stone. Make sure students know what a tombstone is. Provide as many different visuals as possible, as death rituals vary from country to country. Try to include tombstones that have apparent weathering. Then discuss the effects of weathering on the stone in the figure. Have students turn to the person next to them and ask, "What type of weathering probably wore away the letters on the marble tombstone?" Be prepared to discuss their inferences.

Science at Home

Model the suggested activity with the class and strongly urge the students to do this activity at home with other family members. Encourage students to write or illustrate what happens to the clay plugs and to explain what process produces this result. If possible, have them also record remarks from other members of the family.

Assessing the Lesson

Review

Modify the material in the Section 1 Review to accommodate language levels. Give English Language Learners who are not proficient enough to write out complete answers the opportunity to show understanding through diagrams, illustrations, and/or simple phrases and sentences. Or, have students find visuals and configure them in a projectlike presentation or develop an original graphic organizer. The higher-level language students should be able to complete all of the questions, including the Thinking Critically question.

Performance Assessment

After the students have completed the Thinking Critically section and turned in their responses, show a visual of a boulder and have the students who completed this section predict what it will look like in 100 years.

Rate of Weathering

Visitors to New England's historic cemeteries may notice a surprising fact. Slate tombstones from the 1700s are less weathered and easier to read than marble gravestones from the 1800s. Why is this so? **The most important factors that determine the rate at which weathering occurs are type of rock and climate.**

Type of Rock Some kinds of rocks weather more rapidly than others. The minerals that make up the rock determine how fast it weathers. Rock made of minerals that do not dissolve easily in water weathers slowly. Rock made of minerals that dissolve easily in water weathers faster.

Some rock weathers easily because it is permeable. **Permeable** (PUR mee uh bul) means that a material is full of tiny, connected air spaces that allow water to seep through it. Permeable rock weathers chemically at a fast rate. Why? As water seeps through the spaces in the rock, it removes dissolved material formed by weathering.

Climate Climate refers to the average weather conditions in an area. Both chemical and mechanical weathering occur faster in wet climates. Rainfall provides the water needed for chemical changes as well as for freezing and thawing.

Chemical reactions occur faster at higher temperatures. That is why chemical weathering occurs more quickly where the climate is both hot and wet. Granite, for example, is a very hard rock that forms when molten material cools inside Earth. Granite weathers so slowly in cool climates that it is often used as a building stone. But in hot and wet climates, granite weathers faster and eventually crumbles apart.

Figure 3 The rate of weathering of these tombstones depends on the type of rock. Slate (top) resists weathering better than marble (bottom). *Inferring What type of weathering probably wore away the letters on the marble tombstone?*

 Section 1 Review

1. What factors cause mechanical weathering?
2. Describe three causes of chemical weathering.
3. What factors affect the rate of weathering?
4. Explain why chemical weathering occurs faster in hot, wet climates than in cool, dry climates.
5. **Thinking Critically Predicting** Suppose you see a large boulder with several cracks in it. What would you expect to see if you could observe the boulder again in several hundred years? Explain.

Science at Home

Ice in a Straw Here's how to demonstrate one type of weathering for your family. Plug one end of a drinking straw with a small piece of clay. Fill the straw with water. Now plug the top of the straw with clay. Make sure that the clay plugs do not leak. Lay the straw flat in the freezer overnight. Remove the straw the next day. What happened to the clay plugs? What process produced this result? Be sure to dispose of the straw so that no one will use it for drinking.

Science and Society—Preserving Stone Monuments

Before Reading Prepare a world map with the country of Egypt outlined showing the location of the Sphinx. Also outline the United States and the home countries of the English Language Learners. Use the map to reinforce the concept of distance.

During Reading Have students compare the information in the first paragraph with the visual that shows the Sphinx.

After Reading Prepare a chart with three headings: *Should Structures Be Restored? Can New Technology Slow Weathering?* and *What Else Can People Do?* Elicit responses from students after they read each section. Encourage complete sentence answers. Put the responses on the chart and discuss them.

Group students for the *You Decide* section, making sure that all language levels are represented in each group. Have reference books, including books with visuals, available for the students to complete this exercise. Have the groups discuss and record their thoughts about the difficulties in preserving ancient monuments. Provide visuals of ancient monuments that are representative of the home countries of the English Language Learners. Encourage students to make connections about weather, atmospheric conditions, and cultural interpretations of the value of monuments.

Have students divide a piece of paper into two sections. Tell them to label one section *Advantages* and the other *Disadvantages*. Have each group discuss the advantages and disadvantages of using different methods of preserving monuments. Have them make a list of their ideas.

Instruct each group to research a monument and design a plan to preserve it. Tell them that the plan should be an illustration with a written set of plans. Encourage the students to use reference books to identify the monument that they plan to research.

SCIENCE AND SOCIETY

Preserving Stone Monuments

A statue with a human head and a lion's body crouches in the desert beside the pyramids of Egypt. This is the great Sphinx. It was carved out of limestone about 4,500 years ago. Thousands of years of weathering by water, wind, and sand have worn away much of the Sphinx's face. In the 1800s, sand that had protected the Sphinx's body was cleared away. Weathering attacked the newly exposed parts of the Sphinx. Flakes and even chunks of stone fell from the statue. Workers tried to repair the Sphinx with cement. But the repairs weakened the statue and changed its shape.

The Issues

Should Structures Be Restored?
Weathering threatens many ancient stone monuments throughout the world. Pollutants in air and rain make stone weather faster. But there are ways to slow the weathering of a monument without changing or damaging it. In 1998, workers in Egypt completed a new restoration of the Sphinx. They removed the added cement. They replaced the damaged stones with new, hand-cut limestone blocks of the same size and weight. The new stone will help protect what remains of the monument. Visitors to the Sphinx will now see only the original statue and repairs made with original materials. The new repairs preserve the statue's original shape.

Most people want the Sphinx and other monuments to be restored. But restoration is time-consuming and very expensive. And in some cases, repair work can damage or change the original structure.

Can New Technology Slow Weathering?
Advances in technology may provide some solutions. At the Sphinx, scientists measure wind direction, wind speed, and moisture in the air. This information helps scientists follow the weathering process and provides data that will help prevent more damage. Similar instruments are used at other monuments.

Other scientists are working on a way of coating stone with a chemical compound to strengthen and repair the surface. So far, they have found a compound that sticks well to sandstone, but not to marble or limestone.

What Else Can People Do? Repair and restoration are not the only options. Some say that ancient monuments should be buried again after being uncovered by archaeologists. Some people suggest that the Sphinx itself should be reburied in the sand that protected it for so many centuries. But scholars, archaeologists, and tourists disagree. Meanwhile, as people seek solutions, rain, wind, sun, and polluted air continue to take their toll.

You Decide

1. Identify the Problem
In your own words, explain the difficulties involved in preserving ancient monuments.

2. Analyze the Options
List methods for preserving ancient buildings and monuments. Note the advantages and disadvantages of repair work, technology, and other approaches.

3. Find a Solution
Make a plan to preserve a monument in your city. Write your recommendations in the form of a letter to a city mayor or town council.

Sample Lesson: Physical Science
Covalent Bonds

Preparing the Lesson

Assess Prior Knowledge

Complete a review of atoms by having visuals of an atom and a written definition. Ask students to turn to the person sitting next to them and decide on one thing they know about atoms. Write down the responses on the board or chart under the word *Atom*. Repeat the responses correctly and offer some elaboration of responses if needed. As you record the responses, build whatever background is needed for all students to understand this section. Review with the students ionic bonds.

Review the activities completed about ionic bonds and the visuals. Tell the students that in this section they will learn about bonds that atoms form by sharing electrons.

Key Terms

Develop a Word Wall (discussed on page 14) using the key terms *covalent bond*, *double bond*, *molecular compound*, *polar*, and *nonpolar*. Entitle the Word Wall *Covalent Bonds*. Include a visual to represent the meaning of the object, a written definition and break words into parts. For example, in the words *covalent* and *nonpolar*, underline the prefixes *co-*, which means "together," and *non-*, which means "not." Refer to the Word Wall during the instructional sequence and encourage students to use it as a reference when completing assignments.

Discover

To build interest, have students complete the Discover activity, preferably in pairs. After the students observe the reaction of adding soap to vegetable oil and water, have them write their observations and reflections in their science notebooks. English Language Learners who are at a beginning language level should sketch what they observed. Check comprehension by observing and questioning the English Language Learner when the activity is completed.

Reading Tip

Have an illustration of covalent bonds and ionic bonds posted in the room. Group students into pairs and lead them as they write predictions of how they think covalent bonds differ from ionic bonds. Place these predictions next to the illustrations of the

covalent bonds and the ionic bonds. After reading, the students will revisit their predictions to see if they were accurate.

Study and Comprehension

Guide the students through the section of the text by having them complete a modified concept circle. To make a modified concept circle (discussed on page 29), have each student draw a large circle and write *Covalent Bonds* in it. Then tell them to draw lines extending out from the large circle. Instruct students to write the subtitles on the lines in another color. After students complete the concept circle go over the subtitles and give a brief introduction to what the students will learn. Give an example of electron sharing so the students will have a general idea of these concepts. This activity will give you a sense of what the students already know about the subject from their reaction and the level of discussion.

Reading the Lesson

Introduction

Before Reading Have two students demonstrate the following scenario. Give each student 35 cents. Have a sign that says "Apples: 40¢ each or two for 70¢." The class will help the students problem solve the following question: "How can both students buy an apple?" Explain to the students that this type of sharing is connected to electron sharing, which they will study in this section.

Electron Sharing

Before Reading Guide the students to the first subtitle, Electron Sharing. Preview Figure 6 and explain that the shared pair of electrons in a molecule of fluorine forms a single covalent bond. Have an enlargement of Figure 6 available and carefully explain what the visual represents. To reinforce the concept, instruct students to copy this illustration in their science notebooks along with the definition of *covalent bond*.

During Reading Point out two important sentences that will give ELLs the gist of the section:

- A chemical bond formed when two atoms share electrons is called a covalent bond.

- In a covalent bond, both atoms attract the two shared electrons at the same time.

Connect these two sentences with Figure 6 to enhance understanding of the concept. As students read the second paragraph, have them write down the difference between ionic bonds and covalent bonds.

After Reading Encourage explanations and discussion by having additional diagrams or visuals of ionic and covalent bonds available to help English Language Learners understand the differences between them.

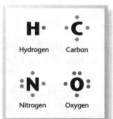

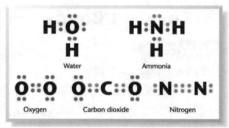

Figure 7 The electron dot diagrams for hydrogen, carbon, nitrogen, and oxygen (left) show the number of valence electrons for each. The diagrams of molecules (right) show how the electrons are shared in covalent bonds.
Interpreting Diagrams How many bonds does each nitrogen atom form?

How Many Bonds?

Look at the electron dot diagrams for oxygen, nitrogen, and carbon atoms in Figure 7. Count the dots on each atom. The number of bonds these atoms can form equals the number of valence electrons needed to make a total of eight.

For example, oxygen has six valence electrons, so it can form two covalent bonds. In a water molecule, oxygen forms one covalent bond with each hydrogen atom. Since nitrogen has five valence electrons, it can form three bonds. In ammonia (NH_3), a nitrogen atom bonds with three hydrogen atoms.

Next, compare water to a molecule of oxygen. Can you find the two covalent bonds? This time *two* pairs of electrons are shared between the oxygen atoms, forming a **double bond**. In a carbon dioxide molecule, carbon forms a double bond with each oxygen atom. Elements such as nitrogen and carbon can even form triple bonds in which *three* pairs of electrons are shared.

Count the electrons around any atom in the molecules in Figure 7. Remember that shared pairs count for both atoms forming a bond. You'll find that each atom has eight valence electrons. The exception is hydrogen, which can have no more than two electrons and forms one bond.

Figure 8 Molecular compounds have much lower melting points than ionic compounds.

Melting and Boiling Points of Some Molecular Compounds			
Compound	Formula	Melting Point (°C)	Boiling Point (°C)
Water	H_2O	0	100
Methane	CH_4	−182	−164
Carbon dioxide	CO_2	—	−78.6*
Ammonia	NH_3	−77.7	−33.6
Rubbing alcohol	C_3H_7OH	−89.5	82.4
Sugar	$C_{12}H_{22}O_{11}$	185–186	(decomposes)

*Carbon dioxide changes directly from a solid to a gas.

Properties of Molecular Compounds

Molecular compounds consist of molecules having covalently bonded atoms. Such compounds have very different properties from ionic compounds.

Look at Figure 8, which lists the melting and boiling points for some molecular compounds. Quite a difference from the

How Many Bonds?

Before Reading Use the diagrams to aid comprehension. Have students look at the first part of Figure 7. Explain what the electron dot diagram shows. Direct them to count the dots on each atom. Make sure students understand what the H, C, N, and O represent. After the students understand the electron dot diagram, move to the diagram of molecules. Explain what this diagram represents and, if necessary, use commonly used words to reinforce meaning and to help all levels of English Language Learners comprehend the concept. Provide additional examples of individual atoms and compounds with double bonds for students.

During Reading Pair the students to find responses to the following statements as they read this section. Have them record their responses in their science notebooks.

1. What is a double bond?

2. Give an example of elements that can form triple bonds.

After Reading Have the students reproduce the diagram in Figure 7 in their student notebooks with an explanation. Taking into consideration their levels of language, you may prefer to have students use modeling clay to replicate the figure and explain orally what they have made.

Properties of Molecular Compounds

Before Reading Choose the most important sentences that relate to the concept being studied and provide those to the students. Guide the students to Figure 8. Interpret the chart for them and tell them the importance of the chart. Ask questions such as the following:

1. What is the formula for sugar?

2. What does *melting point* mean?

3. What is the melting point of ammonia?

4. What does *boiling point* mean?

5. What is the boiling point of methane?

801°C and 1,413°C described for table salt! In molecular solids, the molecules are held close to each other. But the forces holding them are much weaker than those holding ions together in an ionic solid. Less heat is needed to separate molecules than is needed to separate ions. Some molecular compounds, such as sugar and water, do form crystals. But these compounds, like other molecular solids, melt and boil at much lower temperatures than ionic compounds do.

Most molecular compounds are poor conductors of electricity. No charged particles are available to move, and electricity does not flow. That's why molecular compounds, such as plastic and rubber, are used to insulate electric wires. Even as liquids, molecular compounds are poor conductors. Pure water, for example, does not conduct electricity. Neither does water with sugar dissolved in it.

Checkpoint Why are molecular compounds poor conductors?

Unequal Sharing of Electrons

Have you ever played tug of war? If you have, you know that if both teams have equal strength, the contest is a tie. But what if the teams pull on the rope with unequal force? Then the rope moves closer to one side or the other. The same is true of electrons in a covalent bond. **Some atoms pull more strongly on the shared electrons than other atoms do. As a result, the electrons move closer to one atom, causing the atoms to have slight electrical charges.** These charges are not as strong as the charges on ions. But the unequal sharing is enough to make one atom slightly negative and the other atom slightly positive. A covalent bond in which electrons are shared unequally is **polar.**

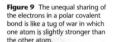

Designing Experiments

Suppose you have samples **ACTIVITY** of two colorless, odorless gases. You are told that one gas is methane (CH_4) and the other is carbon dioxide (CO_2). How could you use the information in Figure 8 to find out which gas is which? Describe the experiment you would set up. Tell what conditions you would control and what you would change. What result would you look for to get an answer?

Figure 9 The unequal sharing of the electrons in a polar covalent bond is like a tug of war in which one atom is slightly stronger than the other atom.

During Reading Orally guide the students through the selection. State the following questions. Then write each one on the board and give students time to find the answers. Discuss the answers, and then have students write the questions and answers in their science notebooks.

1. What are molecular compounds?
2. How are the melting and boiling points for molecular compounds different from those for ionic solids?
3. What are examples of molecular compounds that are poor conductors?
4. How are plastic and rubber used as a consequence of being poor conductors of electricity?

After Reading Help ELLs bring together information to answer the Checkpoint question. Based on Question 4 above, remind them that plastic and rubber are used to insulate wire because they are poor conductors of electricity. Then ask why electricity does not flow through them. Guide students to infer that poor conductors don't contain any available electrons to allow a flow.

Unequal Sharing of Electrons

Before Reading Instruct students to look at Figure 9 and ask if they think that one side could be slightly stronger than the other. Give them the opportunity to discuss their reactions. Call attention to the sentence in bold print. Help students see the connection between the photograph and the definition of *polar*. Direct the students to the last sentence of the first paragraph, which brings the information together in bold print to form the definition of the term *polar*. Have the students enter the definition of *polar* in their science notebooks or glossaries using their own words.

During Reading Since both the main idea sentence and the definition of the word *polar* have been pulled from the paragraph, there is no need for the students to go back to read the paragraph. Often you need only pull important sentences from scientific texts so that English Language Learners get the gist of the material.

After Reading Point out Figure 10, in which the diagram on the left side shows the opposite of polar, *nonpolar*. Explain the two parts of the figure and have the students replicate it in their science notebooks.

Figure 10 In the nonpolar bond in F_2, the two fluorine atoms pull equally on the shared electrons. In the polar bond in HF, fluorine pulls more strongly on the shared electrons than hydrogen does.

If two atoms pull equally on the electrons, neither atom becomes charged. This is the case when the two atoms are identical, as in fluorine gas (F_2). The valence electrons are shared equally and the bond is **nonpolar.** Compare the bond in F_2 with the polar bond in hydrogen fluoride (HF) in Figure 10.

Nonpolar Molecules Keep tug of war in mind as you look at the carbon dioxide (CO_2) molecule in Figure 11. Oxygen attracts electrons much more strongly than carbon, so bonds between oxygen and carbon are polar. But the two oxygen atoms are pulling with equal strength in opposite directions. In a sense, they cancel each other out. Overall, a carbon dioxide molecule is nonpolar even though it has polar bonds. A molecule is nonpolar if it contains polar bonds that cancel each other. As you might guess, molecules that contain only nonpolar bonds are also nonpolar.

Polar Molecules Water molecules are polar. As you can see in Figure 11, the shape of the molecule leaves the two hydrogen atoms more to one end and the oxygen atom toward the other. The oxygen atom pulls electrons closer to it from both hydrogen atoms. Overall, the molecule is polar. It has a slightly negative charge at the oxygen end and a slightly positive charge near the hydrogen atoms.

✓ Checkpoint What makes a covalent bond polar?

Attractions Between Molecules

If you could shrink small enough to move among a bunch of water molecules, what would you find? The negatively charged oxygen ends and positively charged hydrogen ends behave like poles of a bar magnet. They attract the opposite ends of other water molecules. These attractions between positive and negative ends pull water molecules toward each other.

What about carbon dioxide? There is no pulling between these molecules. Remember, carbon dioxide molecules are nonpolar. No oppositely charged ends means there are no strong attractions between the molecules.

Language Arts
CONNECTION

Breaking a word into its parts can help you understand its meaning. Take *covalent*, for example. The prefix *co-* means "together." The *-valent* part comes from "valence electrons." So "valence electrons together" can remind you that in a covalent bond, valence electrons are shared.

In Your Journal

The prefix *co-* is used in many other words—*coauthor*, *coexist*, and *cooperate* are just a few. Add five more *co-* words to this list and try to define them all without looking them up. Then check their meanings in a dictionary and write sentences that use each one.

Language Arts Connection

Refer to the word *covalent* on the Word Wall. Remind students that the prefix *co-* means "together" and the original meaning of the term *valence* was "strength." Relate this to the meaning of *covalent* as describing atoms that combine to share their strength, or their hold on electrons. Make a list of words that begin with the prefix *co-* and their definitions. Students can then choose one word and develop a sentence for their science glossaries.

Attractions Between Molecules

Before Reading To help English Language Learners understand Figure 11, give them an opportunity to replicate the models. Group or pair the students and have them construct their figure from cut-out circles and small squares of paper with plus and minus signs. As they work, explain what the models represent.

During Reading Explain to students that differences in the attractions of polar and nonpolar molecules lead to different properties in compounds. Condense the information in these two paragraphs for easier comprehension.

After Reading Guide the students to go back to the Discover activity at the beginning of the section. Ask what happened when they put water and vegetable oil together. Challenge them to explain this in terms of the lack of attraction between a polar and a nonpolar molecule. Then ask what happened when soap was added. Make sure students understand that soap is a very long molecule that has one polar end and one nonpolar end. Challenge them to understand how this affects its attraction to dirt.

Assessing the Lesson

Review

As an alternative review for English Language Learners whose language level is not advanced or transitional, you can adapt Check Your Progress and let students replicate one of the figures that has been taught. Once students have completed the models, have them provide an explanation of each one at their level of understanding and writing in English.

For the Thinking Critically question, allow students to visually represent the comparison and contrasting of the covalent bond and ionic bond. The use of a Venn diagram (Transparency 7) will clarify the differences and similarities between a covalent bond and an ionic bond.

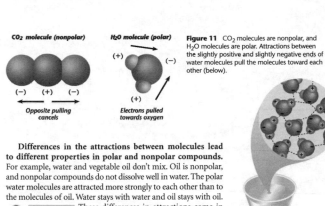

CO₂ molecule (nonpolar)   H₂O molecule (polar)

(+)   (−)

(−) (+) (−)   (+)

Opposite pulling cancels   *Electrons pulled towards oxygen*

Figure 11 CO_2 molecules are nonpolar, and H_2O molecules are polar. Attractions between the slightly positive and slightly negative ends of water molecules pull the molecules toward each other (below).

Differences in the attractions between molecules lead to different properties in polar and nonpolar compounds. For example, water and vegetable oil don't mix. Oil is nonpolar, and nonpolar compounds do not dissolve well in water. The polar water molecules are attracted more strongly to each other than to the molecules of oil. Water stays with water and oil stays with oil.

INTEGRATING TECHNOLOGY These differences in attractions come in handy when you wash laundry. Many kinds of dirt—for example, grease—are nonpolar compounds. Their molecules won't mix with plain water. So how can you wash dirt out of your clothes?

As you found if you did the Discover activity, adding soap helped the oil and water to mix. When you do laundry, detergent causes the nonpolar dirt to mix with the polar water. Soaps and detergents have long molecules. One end of a soap molecule is polar, and the other end is nonpolar. Soaps and detergents dissolve in water because the polar ends of their molecules are attracted to water molecules. Meanwhile, their nonpolar ends mix easily with the dirt. When the water washes down the drain, the soap and the dirt go with it.

Section 2 Review

1. How are valence electrons involved in the formation of a covalent bond?
2. How do atoms in covalent bonds become slightly negative or slightly positive?
3. Explain how attractions between molecules could cause water to have a higher boiling point than carbon dioxide.
4. **Thinking Critically Comparing and Contrasting** In terms of electrons, how is a covalent bond different from an ionic bond?

Check Your Progress   CHAPTER PROJECT

Use your materials to build molecules with single covalent bonds. Also make models of molecules containing double or triple bonds. (*Hint:* After you make bonds, each atom should have a total of eight valence electrons or, in the case of hydrogen, two valence electrons.)